DEVELOPING IN THE DARK

Standing on the Promise while Going through the Process

Dear Jackie,

    You are so precious to me ♡

My prayer for you is as you read
the account of my life in these pages,
God will show up in a personal way.
He is, and always will be all that
you need. Always Agape ♡

Marilyn Beattie

Marilyn

Jer 29: 11

ISBN 979-8-88943-923-3 (paperback)
ISBN 979-8-88943-924-0 (digital)

Christian Faith Publishing
832 Park Avenue
Meadville, PA 16335
www.christianfaithpublishing.com

All biblical citations were taken from the King James Version of the Holy Bible unless otherwise indicated.

Printed in the United States of America

Contents

Acknowledgments

I WANT TO START BY THANKING MY darling husband, David. You have shown me what true love looks like. You have been here with me through this entire writing process. You have heard all these stories multiple times, yet you remain patient while I recall them again. Thank you for allowing me to read you excerpts while you prepared for work, ate breakfast or lunch, or chilled out in bed. You lovingly handed me tissues while I wept as I read the words written on these pages. You laughed with me and prayed with me. Your heart of compassion and your words of encouragement and support are priceless treasures, and I honor and adore you.

My precious daughter, Angela, you have walked this road with me. Together, we have laughed, cried, and prayed our way through countless tough times.

You have wisdom beyond your years. I want to thank you for your strength, for your encouragement, for believing in me, for being my travel companion, for singing silly songs in the middle of the night as we traveled, for being a bright spot during a very dark time in my life. You are, and will always be, my treasure!

To God, my words fail to show my gratitude for all You have brought me through and all You have taught me. Thank You for not giving up on me. Thank You for the lessons learned in the darkroom. Would I want to do it all over again? No, I would not, but I am so grateful to have You, my Lord and Savior, as my companion on this remarkable journey. I am here today, only by Your grace. Thank You for surrounding me with Your presence, for teaching me Your ways, for imparting Your rich wisdom into my spirit. Thank You for developing me so that I may be counted mature enough to carry the anointing that You have me walk in. To You, the only wise God, I give all praise, honor, and glory forever and ever. Amen.

Foreword

To all who open these pages:

You will not be able to put Marilyn's book down! Once you begin, you will find every chapter and ending keeps you captured with bated breath; "What could possibly happen next?"

I was privileged to be Marilyn's pastor during the 1980s in Mifflinburg, Pennsylvania. She was raised by wonderful parents who were committed to God and the church. My acquaintance with Marilyn began in some therapy sessions where she struggled to gain spiritual victory over the resentful feelings she had toward her mother-in-law. During that time, she sang and played with the group called Forgiven. At times, when I was asked to serve as an evangelist around the area, Forgiven was often asked to serve as the song evangelists for the campaign. Marilyn was a blessing. She wrote numerous songs and gave personal testimonies that lifted hearts. The lyrics to her song, "One Day, One Hour, One Moment," were dropped into her spirit while I preached a sermon by that very same title on a Sunday morning at our church. The message of that song, as well as many others that she has written, has been a blessing to the many churches and audiences she and Forgiven sang to. Obviously, as you gain knowledge of her through her recounting in these pages, you will find her life was a roller coaster of light and darkness, ups and downs, unbelievable and believable. But in it all, God was shaping, forming, and developing the beautiful person she is today.

As you read her life story, you will, as I did, discover moments of unbelief as well as be able to identify with her days of spiritual weakness, defeat, and emotional pain. There can be only one conclusion. In Marilyn, God was, has been, and still is making a beautiful work on His potter's wheel.

Pastor Dave West

Introduction

EVERY LIFE HAS A STORY THAT NEEDS to be told. Every person has a voice that needs to be heard. Every life has intrinsic value. Every soul is worth redeeming. Sometimes, it takes a lifetime to learn the truth of these statements. Such is the case with this book. This story, my story, has been years in the making. My desire to tell my story in written format began many years ago when my marriage was young, but God did not want me to write it then. He knew that I would not be writing for the right reasons.

This is my story—the good, the bad, and the ugly truth! To some, it will come as a shock, to others it will serve as confirmation of what they knew all along. To me, it is a necessary part of my healing journey on my way to wholeness. To God be all glory, honor, and praise. He has kept me, sustained me, strengthened me, empowered me, and enabled me to survive. He put me in a dark place, isolated, on a shelf, in a far corner, and as the dust of life gathered around me, He lovingly and tenderly developed me. He developed my character, my level of maturity, my understanding; He developed the fruit of His Spirit in me, He put me in a place of humility, He disciplined me with love, grace, and mercy.

The human side of me wants to hide the ugly truth and the shame that comes with it. The temptation to embellish my story in order to paint me in the best light is very real. In order to resist that temptation and put it away from me, I need to be truthful, authentic, and transparent, and face the shame and regret head-on.

This is a story of God developing me in the darkroom. Every word is true to the best of my ability to recall. Sometimes, details in events can become lost in the passage of time. Much prayer has gone into the writing of this book. My heart's cry is that, through me sharing the painful journey of my life here in these pages, someone will be encouraged to press on. Maybe you are reading this book, and you can relate to my story on so many levels. I am glad you found this book. God has a message for you here. It is a message of hope, a message of His faithfulness, a message that says you have great value, a message that says He sees you, He knows you, and He has a plan for your life.

Just recently, God has spoken into my life through a prophetic word, that He is getting ready to bring me out into the light in new ways that I never dreamed possible. New doors of ministry will be opening up, my gifts go before me to prepare the way. God has released in me the desire to share my story now at this point in my life. He says I am ready to share it with the world, and now it will be told for all the right reasons. This book is the launching pad for the new adventure that God has been preparing me for all along. He is ready to have me emerge from the darkroom and come bursting into the "Son-light" of His glorious LOVE! Let's go!

CHAPTER 1

Not Your Average Child

A YOUNG HUSBAND AND WIFE, ALONG WITH their two small daughters, were eking out an existence on a rented farm in Central Pennsylvania. The soil was overladen with rock, and much labor went into preparing the ground to produce enough crops to feed them and their herd of dairy cattle. Each year, in early spring, the ground would be plowed, and innumerable limestone rocks appeared to the point where the fields appeared whitish gray in color. The young farmer was a very determined man and wanted to be successful, no matter how labor-intensive it was. So, after plowing the ground, the family would spend days in the fields, picking the rocks

1

by hand, one at a time, and throwing them onto a flatbed wagon where they would be taken to a large sinkhole on the property and thrown off the wagon, again by hand. It was hard work. It required a lot of time and was challenging in that the more rocks they removed, the more rocks showed up. This was an exhausting cycle that continued for as long as the land was farmed.

Theirs was a godly faith founded on biblically sound principles and reinforced by daily family Bible reading and prayer. This was known as "family altar" time. It was here that the family shared scripture, usually read by the husband, sometimes a hymn or song would be sung, and fellowship among the family members was precious. Prayer was always corporate, meaning that everyone knelt by a chair or sofa and prayed out loud at the same time. You might be thinking to yourself, that sounds a bit confusing, but our great and wonderful God hears each and every one of our utterances. He sees each tear, He is acquainted with each sigh, and His heart is touched when we call on His name. It doesn't matter if we are praying alone or with a corporate group; God sees each one individually, and He hears each one individually, all at the same time, whether in a single room or all around the world.

It was in this family that I was born in the spring of 1957, a very busy time on the farm. My parents didn't slow down just because I was born. In fact, when I was just ten days old, my mother took me with her into the fields and held me in her arms as she drove the tractor and planted corn. Thus began my life as the third daughter, the middle child, of a Pennsylvania farming family. After several years, two more daughters would be added to the mix, making us a family of seven members. Yes, my dad was a farmer with five daughters, no sons. We learned, very early in life, the value of hard work, what it means to be a team player, and the satisfaction of a job well done.

My parents were both raised in strict homes. My dad was the oldest child of a Pentecostal pastor. He grew up in parsonages where holy living was mandatory. Rules and regulations were plentiful, and the penalty for disobeying was swift and sure. My mother was the youngest of two children. Her parents, a farming couple, also lived by very legalistic standards. Both sets of grandparents had a no-nonsense approach toward God, church attendance, obeying and honoring God, your parents or anybody else in authority, prayer and Bible reading, excelling in school, and so on.

Both of my parents lived by the same guidelines for me and my sisters. There were times when they would relax a bit and allow us to have some fun, but, for the most part, my childhood was filled with hard work. We never took a family vacation, and prior to marriage, I had never been outside of the state of Pennsylvania. I guess you could say I lived a sheltered life. As I look back on it from this vantage point, I can say that our life was very similar to *Little House on the Prairie.* We lived by a very strict dress code, and standards of conduct were rigid and enforced.

In our home, church attendance was never negotiable. The rule was if the church doors are open, we would be there. Even when I was not feeling well, I was taken to church. I remember feeling too bad to sit up on the pew, so Mom laid me on the hardwood floor at her feet and covered me with her sweater. We attended a little country church that was part of a legalistic denomination of churches. We were forbidden to cut our hair, wear jewelry of any kind, wear makeup, or wear slacks. We were required to wear long sleeves, long dresses, long hair (and it had to be up on our head in a bun-type fashion, not hanging down). Many rules, many regulations led to much judgment of those who did not follow our standards. As far back as I can remember, I questioned what I heard from the pulpit or what I observed from fellow parishioners. I was surrounded by people who were dressed in what they would consider holy attire, but their actions, their conversations, and their attitudes did not always reflect God's character.

As soon as I was able to read, I became an avid student of the Word of God. I would dissect the pastor's message, week after week. My older sister questioned me one Sunday as I spent the afternoon searching the Scriptures to discover truth. She asked me why I couldn't just accept what our pastor said and leave it at that. But I had to know for myself what the Word of God says. So I read the Bible and prayed as a child, seeking the truth with all my heart.

Ours was a musical family. Even while my parents were engaged to be married, they traveled around the area and sang together in revivals, camp meetings, and tent meetings. After they were married, they continued to sing together in churches. As their family grew, they incorporated each one of us into the music ministry. We usually sang more in the summer months when camp meetings and tent meetings were held.

According to my mom, when I was born, the doctor who helped bring me into this world looked me over and told my mom that I was going to be a singer. Mom asked him how he knew that, and he said it was because of the shape of the roof of my mouth. Even at my birth, God used that doctor to speak a prophetic word. His words would prove to be correct.

As a little girl, I had a deep desire to know God in a more profound and personal way. Church made Him seem so far away and unapproachable, so strict and foreboding, but when I studied the Bible for myself, He came alive in my heart. I had a sense of sin, of right and wrong, as far back as I could remember. I had heard countless messages on the second coming of Christ, on the horrors of hell, the joys of heaven, the wages of sin, the rigid standard of holiness in attire, the necessity of sanctification, and the ramifications of rejecting Jesus Christ as Lord and Savior.

I developed speech later in life than some children do. I was still not talking after I reached my second birthday. My mother thought there was something wrong with me, so she made an appointment with our local doctor who took a thorough look at me. He assured Mom that there was nothing wrong with me and that I was very observant, taking it all in, and when I was ready, I would start talking.

Well, he was right! I started speaking in whole sentences, completely bypassing the normal baby babbling, and I threw my parents for a loop. Not only did I speak in entire sentences, but I began preaching. In our home, we had a stairway that led from the kitchen to the upstairs. I would line that stairway with toys, objects, soup cans, bottles of shampoo, bars of soap, rolled-up pairs of socks, shoes, boots, anything that could stay on the steps, and I would stand on the bottom landing and preach to my make-believe congregation. I found a map of Pennsylvania, hung it on the wall at the bottom of the stairs, and pretended that it was a map of Africa. I told anyone within earshot that God had called me to be a missionary, and that when the time was right, I would be going to the mission field. Yes, before I was four years old, I felt the urgency of the call of God to ministry in my life! My mother tells the story of how one day I was in the stairway preaching, and she fell under the Holy Ghost conviction and had tears flowing down her cheeks as she prayed for forgiveness in her own life. She was saved and had a relationship with God, but through something that I said during my "sermon," the Holy

Spirit convicted her, and she repented right there in our kitchen. I had no idea of that happening until many years later.

I remember when missionaries would come and speak at our church a few times each year. I would sit on the front row because I wanted to hear every word. I would sit there, listening to their stories, and imagine myself being on the mission field with them. Their stories became my stories. I told God that I was completely surrendered and prepared to be a missionary, but, in spite of that, I never felt a specific call for me to be a missionary. I did, however, feel a call to ministry that was undeniable.

At four years of age, I had a burning desire to be able to play piano. My mother played, and she was our church pianist. I admired that about her so much, and I wanted to play like she did. One day, I was bugging her to teach me to play the piano. She was busy in the kitchen, and I was persistent about her teaching me to play the piano right then. She was standing at the stove, making dinner. She turned to me and told me that she was too busy to teach me, but if I asked God to help me play the piano, He would. Well, that was good enough for me.

We had a large, black upright grand piano with a stool that one could adjust by winding it up or down. I ran into the room where the piano was, turned the stool down far enough for me to climb up on, placed my two hands on the keys, and prayed a simple prayer that was something like this: "Dear Jesus, I want to play the piano. I asked Mommy to teach me how to play, but she is too busy right now to teach me. She told me that I should ask You to help me to play the piano. So, Jesus, if You teach me how to play this piano, I will play always for You and only for You." I began to move my fingers, and music started to come from that piano. I was playing with two hands! I remember the song as if it were yesterday. It was a hymn that we had sung at church many times called "Under the Atoning Blood of the Lamb."

My mom forgot all about what she was making on the stove and came running into the piano room. She grabbed me off that piano stool and ran with me around the kitchen table, laughing and crying at the same time. I didn't realize the extent of the miracle that had just taken place until later in life. In my childish mind, it was perfectly normal to pray and ask God to do something and then fully expect Him to do what I had asked Him to do. From that day to this, every note that I play on the piano is a gift from God. I have never been able to learn to read music, even though I tried on numerous occasions, with tears and frustration. I know that God has given me the ability to play piano, and He gets all the credit. All the glory goes to Him! There is a holy anointing on my hands, and when I play, the Holy Spirit ministers through the music. I take no credit at all for that. I am simply the instrument in the hands of the Master, and I thank God for this precious gift He has given me so many years ago and continues to bless, even to this very day.

So I grew up in a legalistic home and attended a legalistic church. All the while, God was calling me to ministry, but I was not fully aware of what that meant. I acted it out by preaching to my dolls, studying the Bible, preparing invisible sermons, and making up songs, which I would sing to my stairway congregation. I preached to the cats and kittens in the barn. I preached to our chickens in the henhouse. I preached to the pigs in our pigpen and even preached to the cows as they grazed in the pasture. I preached to our collie dog, Lassie, and she listened. I felt with great urgency the importance of our entire household to know who Jesus is, including all of our animals.

Sundays at our house were very special. They were days set aside from the normal work of the farm, with church attendance both morning and evening, and rest throughout the day. As a child, I did not want to rest. I wanted to play, to ride bike, to go for walks, to play games, anything but rest. My parents welcomed that day of rest because they were exhausted from the toils of life, and they needed to renew their strength for the week ahead. We were allowed to read a book, only if it were preapproved by them. Often, after the noon meal was over, and the dishes were done, I would go to my bedroom, lie on my bed, and read my Bible. I love reading the Word of God, for it is alive, it is quick and powerful, it is God's love letter to my soul. God met with me there, and I gained much knowledge and wisdom in those hours spent with Him in His Word.

Eventually, I came to realize the awesome responsibility of the call of God on my life and began to shift my focus to preparing for a life of service to Almighty God in whatever capacity He chose. I was determined to serve Him with my life.

CHAPTER 2

A Reality Check

WHEN ONE IS LIVING IN THE MOMENT, it is easy to lose sight of what is happening. That has been my experience. God placed a call for ministry on my life. I was aware of it but somehow assumed that it would just happen, things would simply fall into place, and it would just flow. After all, I was God's child, and it was His plan.

The reality is that, as much as God had a plan for my life, the enemy of my soul, Satan, also had a plan. He was determined to undermine, to stop, to hinder, to thwart all of God's plans for my life. He comes to steal, kill, and destroy (John 10:10). His focus was to steal my destiny, to kill my calling, and to destroy my future. And he would use anybody to accomplish that.

I was six years old and about to begin first grade. I could hardly wait! Our farm was situated right behind the town, so I walked to school. I knew only one kid from school, the son of the owners of the little country store in town. We would periodically go there for things like flour, sugar, and bread; oh, and penny candy if Mom gave us an extra nickel. And that's how I knew their son. Other than that, I knew no town kids.

The first day of school arrived, and I took my lunch, kissed my mom, and headed out the door. I was wearing a new dress that my mom had made, and I had on a new pair of shoes. My hair was neatly combed into two long braids, and I felt confident that I was going to really enjoy going to school. My heart was full of expectancy. Oh, the things I would learn! I determined to be the best student possible. I was going to sit still and listen to my teacher, I was going to apply myself and study hard, and I was going to do all my homework.

By the end of the first day, I was convinced that this was going to be a good journey through the next twelve years of my education. But trouble was waiting just outside the doors of the school. As I began walking toward my home, two girls from my class started to follow me. I didn't know them previously but had just met them at recess that very day. They lived in town and were first cousins to each other. At first, they started calling me Amish because of the way I looked. I told them that I was a Christian. Thinking that I had satisfied their curiosity, I expected them to accept that and be my friends. I guess my answer stirred something up inside of them because they began calling me all sorts of names, telling me I looked stupid, and where did I get my clothes anyway? These two girls were dressed in the finest that the stores had to offer at the time. When I told them that my mom made my dress, they accused me all the more of being Amish. I have no problem being called Amish, and I have great respect for people from that culture! They are some of the most hardworking folks that I know.

But the way these girls sneered when they said it made me feel like they hated me. It made me feel dirty and unacceptable. Then they picked up stones and began hurling them at me. I picked up my pace to escape their bullying as tears ran down my face. I was hurt, confused, and scared. I had no idea why they hated me. I didn't even know them. Just as I reached the street that led to the driveway to our farm, both girls took hold of me and told me that if I didn't bring them candy the next day, they would beat me up! I was terrified. I remember going home and frantically searching through the kitchen cupboards, trying to find some candy that I could give them the next day. My mom noticed and asked me what I was searching for. I told her what had just happened to me and that I needed to take them some candy the next day or I would get beat up. Mom informed me that under no circumstances would she allow me to take candy for those two. I tried to prepare myself for what I would face the next day!

The second day of school came, and the joy and expectation that I had felt the day before had been replaced by dread. Fear had crept in and left me feeling uneasy and unprepared. I had no candy for those girls, and I believed they would follow through with their threat. Slowly, I made my way down the driveway to the street that would take me toward the school. To my horror, at the bottom of the street, those two girls were waiting for me. I thought about turning around and returning home, but I knew they saw me so I continued toward them. I thought perhaps they had changed their minds and decided that I could be their friend after all. But the closer I got to them, the more I realized that they were not in the mood to be friendly. They began calling out for their candy, and I started to think about how I was going to get out of the situation without bodily harm. I caught up to where they were waiting and passed right by without a word. They realized that I did not bring them candy, and they shoved me to the ground.

When I fell, I injured my knee and tore a hole in my white stockings. My dress was dirty, my stockings were torn, my knee was hurting, and my heart was broken. Seeing my injuries, they walked away and hurried to school ahead of me. I picked myself up, brushed the dirt off of my dress, gathered my thoughts, and proceeded to the school. I determined to act like nothing had happened. I was preparing a story to tell my mother about how my stockings got torn. Those two girls threatened and bullied me for the entire time that we went to school together, and I never figured out why they hated me so much.

I now believe that they were part of the enemy's plan to attack me. Satan saw me, he saw my heart, he heard me praying and worshipping God, he watched me as I dug into God's Word, and he was all too familiar with the gifts God had blessed me with. He was there when God performed the miracle of teaching me how to play piano, and he stood by and listened as I preached in the stairway to my "congregation," and he hated me. The enemy hated everything that I was, but even more, he hated everything that he knew God had called me to be. Over the course of my life, he would use anybody he could to chip away at my faith, to dim my hope, and to steal my God-given destiny.

In spite of the mistreatment, I managed to get good grades and won the respect of my teacher whom I adored. One day, she went around the classroom and asked each one of us to share with the class what we wanted to be when we grew up. I had no problem telling her what I wanted to be. I told her I was going to be a teacher on a mission field. She was impressed and seemed to beam at the thought of me wanting to be a teacher. But that is exactly who God gifted me to be. I am a teacher, a preacher, an encourager, and instructor from birth. My answer brought giggles and sneers from the class, and from that day, I was alienated even more from the student body. I cannot forget the hateful comments, the name-calling, the ganging up of my peers. I used to say back to them, "Sticks and stones may break my bones, but words will never hurt me."

That is a lie. Words are powerful. The Bible tells us in Proverbs 18:21 that the power of death and life are in the tongue. Even though I kept up an appearance of being fine, the truth is their words left me reeling inside. I began to doubt myself, my faith, my calling. I thought that perhaps if I would try to please them more, the abuse would stop, but I could never do enough. I would carry their books, do their homework, give them answers to test questions, even share my lunch with them if Mom had packed something really good like chocolate cake, apple pie, or some homemade cookies. The more I gave in to them, the more the bullying increased. It was like pouring gasoline on a fire. I could never do enough! The enemy's plan was playing out, but God was faithful to me. He kept me by His grace.

My teacher was my best friend, and I spent a lot of recess time hanging out with her while she graded papers or prepared for the next part of the day. And we talked. We talked about my dreams of being a teaching missionary, and she encouraged me to follow that dream. She made a huge impact on my life, and I will never forget her. Today, sixty years later, I can still recall her gentle nature, her willing spirit, and her words of wisdom as she told me to never stop pursuing the dream that God had placed in my heart.

When I was in fifth grade, our family moved to a farm in another county, a different school district. God has made me an optimist, and I imagined that moving to a different school would be the end of the bullying that I had endured for the past five years. I was being given a second chance at really enjoying going to school. To me, it seemed like a good chance for a new beginning.

Mom drove me to the new school that first day. We went to the office where I was registered and given the books and materials needed for grade five, and somebody from the office led me to my class. This was in March. So much of the school year was behind us. The teacher had told the class that a new student would be joining them shortly, and when I walked in and was introduced to them, one of the guys from the back of the room shouted, "Oh no, a girl!"

Another boy yelled out and said, "Oh no, a stupid girl!" The class erupted in laughter, and I was given a seat in the front row. I heard whispers and giggles. I felt the stares of the entire class on my back. This was not going as I had hoped, and I had been in the new school for less than an hour.

My heart was crushed, and my hopes of having a fresh new start in a new place were dashed upon the rocks. Somehow, I found the strength to endure what lay ahead, but I certainly did not enjoy it. And the enemy's plan to crush me continued to play out.

Girls form cliques at a very young age, and I did not fit in with any of them. So I was a loner all through school, never made friends, and spent a lot of time alone, talking to God, and dreaming of the day when all of this would be behind me, and I could get on with the really important things in life, which were serving God in ministry and making the most of the gifts that He had placed inside of me.

I attended public school for eight trying years, where I was alienated, mistreated, misunderstood, and bullied by fellow students. They thought I was weird because of the way I dressed and the fact that I could not cut my hair or wear makeup or jewelry. Gym class was a big deal because we were required to wear uniforms that included either slacks or shorts. I could not wear either of those, so my mom wrote an excuse for me to sit out of that class. In place of gym class, I was required to go to a study hall and read books and do lots of book reports. The same thing happened when we were taught square dancing. Since we were never permitted to dance, I was excused from that as well, which only served to heighten the teasing, the ridiculing, the name-calling. I hated going to school and even developed physical problems as a result of the stress of being bullied.

In the summer between grade eight and nine, I asked my parents if I could attend a Bible school not too far from our home. It was not free. In fact, it cost a lot of money to go there, but I knew that God had placed a call for ministry on my life, and I wanted to pursue a Christian education so that I could make the most of what God had placed inside me. My desire was to hone the skills, sharpen the gifts, and be the best representative for my God as I could possibly be. I wanted to serve Him with all my heart, mind, soul, and strength. At first, they were hesitant, but as the summer wore on, my dread of returning to public school intensified, and my persistence won out. My mom took me to get registered at the Bible school, and I could hardly wait for the rest of my life to begin! At last, I could attend school with people who were like-minded. What a huge difference that was going to make.

This Bible school is owned and operated by the legalistic denomination of churches I had attended as a child. It seems that there should be no issues whatsoever. However, previous to me enrolling as a student, our family left that legalistic church and were attending a nondenominational church elsewhere. Unbeknownst to me, that fact alone set me up for something that I was not prepared for at all—to be bullied! This time, the bullying would not come from fellow students but, rather, from the school principal.

Each morning, while we filed into the school, the principal would greet us with a yardstick in his hand with which he measured the length of our skirts. They were measured from the ground up, and we were given a limit of six inches from the floor, no matter how high the heels on our shoes. I was experiencing a growth spurt, and my dresses were a bit short for the standards of the Bible school. So from the first day, I was singled out as a rebel, and looked down on as noncompliant. And the fact that my parents no longer attended one of the churches from that legalistic denomination further placed me in a position of disadvantage. I was an outsider.

As a ninth grader, I had become all too familiar with the cruelty that was measured out to me by my fellow students. I began that first year at the Bible school with a new fervor. I was even accepted, for the most part, by the student body who looked exactly like me. How awesome it would be to get an education in a Christian environment without the concerns of verbal, physical, and psychological attack. Within the first week of attending the Bible school, I received a wake-up call that would be a turning point in my life. The reality is people can be cruel, no matter where or when, and the enemy will use them to the fullest extent that he can.

The Bible school principal was not a kind man at all. He always seemed to be angry about something and was lacking in the area of grace and mercy. Day after day, I would walk into the school, and day after day, I would be met with his yardstick, which he bounced off the floor as we girls all stepped up to have the length of our skirts measured. Lots of mornings, he would pull me out of line and tell me to go to his office and wait for him. Once the school day began, he would come into his office and lecture me on how I was not living up to the standards of the school, even threatening to have me removed from the school, so I could not attend class until I complied. He made me stand in front of a full-length mirror while he lectured me on how inappropriately I was dressed. He made me sit on a chair in front of that mirror, cross and uncross my legs, all the while pointing out how dreadful I looked. He made me stand up and bend over to touch my toes to see how far up my skirt went on the back of my legs, and he yelled at me to comply to the standards. He would make me write for the entire school day these words: "I will wear longer skirts."

One day, he shoved a dress pattern in my face, told me to learn how to sew, and said I needed to make some skirts that were acceptable. Ninth grade was difficult for me on so many levels, and I prayed a lot, just to be able to make it through that experience. The entire school was required to attend chapel services three times a week. I hung out at the altar a lot, crying out to God for the strength to endure. The joy and peace that I had anticipated in that Bible school environment was not realized, and I settled in to a routine of doing what was required of me to get good grades. When that school year came to a close, I felt intense relief that I had the summer before me where I could get a respite from the critical eye and hostile disposition of that man.

I began grade ten with a new determination. My heart cried out to learn more of God, to see His glory in my life, and to walk in the calling wherewith God had called me. I kept telling myself that this year would be better than the last. I prayed frequently throughout the summer months that the principal would find peace in his life and experience the joy of knowing Jesus in a personal way. I was intentional about my own relationship with Jesus Christ and deeply desired to learn all that I could about Him in an environment that encouraged personal growth in every area. I wanted to be taught deep, hidden truths that live in the Word of God. I longed to learn more about how to grow in wisdom, understanding, knowledge, and anointing. I was eager to become the woman of God that I was divinely destined to be.

My hopes, dreams, desires, and anticipations were quickly dashed on the very first day of grade ten, for there, right inside the front door, was the principal with the same yardstick bouncing loudly off the floor as he measured the length of all our skirts. Wow, here we go again! I determined to settle into a routine of learning, pressing into the presence of God. This is the year I would turn sixteen. This is when I would learn to drive and get a driver's license. I was excited at that thought. As I faced the angry principal each morning, I would not make eye contact with him but kept my face turned downward, hoping that he would just let me pass and go on to my class. Some days, it worked, and some days, he would yell abruptly at me to look him in the eye. What I saw in that gaze was not goodness, graciousness, or mercy. I saw anger, frustration, and a whole lot of pride.

Thinking about him now, in the light of all that has transpired in my life, I believe he was narcissistic and had never fully surrendered to the lordship of Jesus Christ. It is one thing to trust in Jesus as your Savior who forgives you, redeems you from death, and washes your soul white in the blood of the Lamb. But it is another realm completely to submit, to surrender, to yield to Him, making Him Lord of your life. And if Jesus Christ is not Lord OF ALL, He cannot be Lord AT ALL. There are no exceptions. We cannot serve God as Lord while still wanting to hold onto the reigns of our will. Stubborn pride must be crucified. Pride will always pit us against the lordship of Jesus Christ. Pride will separate us from His will. Pride is a sin that God says He hates. Hate is a strong word, and God says He hates it. I don't know of anything that is stronger language or that carries more weight than that. Read about the list of seven things that God hates in Proverbs 6:16–19.

One morning, I arrived at school to face the yardstick. This day, I was wearing a long black skirt that buttoned from top to bottom. It had a waistband that was not elastic or stretchy at all. I was thin and fit, and the skirt fit snuggly around my small waist. But there was a problem. The length was just a bit short. The principal was not in a good mood at all that day. In fact, it seemed like he was angry at the whole world. He bellowed and snorted at the girls ahead of me in line, and I prepared myself to step into the invisible circle on the floor as the measure of judgment was made. The girl ahead of me passed his rigid inspection, and he yelled, "Next!" I stepped forward.

There was an elderly instructor standing in the hall that morning. She was nice and kind and carried a spirit of grace and mercy. She was asked by the principal to stand by and be a witness to the measuring process. Sometimes, there would be a woman instructor. Sometimes, it would be a man instructor who witnessed the ritual. As soon as my skirt met the yardstick, the principal yelled, "Unacceptable!" With that, he dropped the yardstick, took both of his hands, grabbed my skirt, and yanked! The three top buttons popped off, and my skirt fell in a puddle at my feet! There I stood in my long white slip while all the male students passed by single file on their way into the school. These male students ranged in age from kindergarten to college seniors. Oh, the males did not have to pass by the judgment seat of measurement because they did not wear skirts. So I was standing there in total shock and humiliation, my skirt laying in a heap at my feet, my white slip exposed, and male students of all ages parading past. And I was nearly sixteen years old! It was quite a scene!

The principal immediately began yelling at the female instructor, "Do something! Do something!" She flew into action, reached down and gathered my skirt, pulling it up awkwardly around me, and hurried me into the office, and closed the door. I was not only embarrassed, hurt, and shaken, but I was downright angry! The female instructor left me standing in the office while she went into the hallway to retrieve the three buttons that had been torn off my skirt. She returned with them and made an attempt to fasten them with pins. When that didn't work, she just pinned my skirt and handed me the three buttons, and told me to get to class.

I had no idea how to face my fellow students. Something inside of me changed that day. It was like a switch had been thrown. I knew my time inside the walls of that school was done. My dream of getting a biblically based education was dead. I was done. The principal had unknowingly been used by Satan to destroy my faith, rob my hope, and kill my dream. It has been said that man can live without many things, but man cannot live without hope. My hopes of ever graduating from Bible school and then continuing on in four years of college at the same school died that day.

Every child has endless value placed on them by our great Creator, God! If you are blessed with a position to work with these unique individuals, consider yourself favored by God, for He searches for special people to teach and train up our children. Only God knows what He has packed inside each child, only He knows their destiny, only He gets to decide where they will be called, planted, groomed, and grown. And if you are a part of that process, you will be blessed as well.

I know that working with youth can be challenging at times, and they can get on your last nerve. But please hear me when I tell you that they have eternal value, and how we value them is a direct reflection of how we value God. Children act out for various reasons, and, often, we do not know their whole story; what their homelife is like, what negative influences they are exposed to, what abuse they suffer, what dysfunction reigns in their home. Our role is to love them as much as God does, even with all their baggage.

In my opinion, if you are not compassionate and patient, possessing lots of loving-kindness and long-suffering, combined with perseverance, you have no business in any occupation that involves children or youth, period. Our children are one of our most priceless resources, for they are our future. We need to protect them with all that is in us to do so.

My focus shifted with that experience in the hallway that morning when the principal literally yanked my skirt off me. The desire I had to get a Christian education was completely gone! I could not stand to look at him, much less come under his authority every single day for the next six years! Yes, six more years under him was just too much to comprehend; two more years of high school followed by four years of college. No, it was not going to happen. My goal now was to figure out a way of escape!

CHAPTER 3

The Trap Is Set

My pastor approached me on a Sunday morning at our church. He told me that he was working on his schedule of events for the year, and one of those events was a series of meetings known as revival. He asked me to serve as song evangelist. I was thrilled. This was different. I grew up in a musical family. We sang as a family locally. We had three different trios in the mix; different combinations of family members, and what a delight it was to blend our voices in three-part harmony!

But now my pastor was requesting me to stand alone and minister and lead the people in worship. I would be turning sixteen years old in a few months, and this was a big deal for me. I always knew that

God had a place in ministry for me, and I was ready to step up and serve Him with all my heart. I said, "Yes, I would be delighted to be the song evangelist." I could hardly wait! I just wanted to walk in my calling, for there is nothing like it on the earth. There is nowhere I would rather be than in the center of God's will, surrounded by His glory, under His anointing, filled with and led by His Holy Spirit.

The revival was scheduled for ten nights, beginning on a Friday evening and running over two Sundays. I was all in! I sang and played to the glory of God. It was heaven on earth for me to be walking in the place that had been ordained by God. Life was good, God was great, and my dream of a lifetime of ministry had been rekindled from the ashes. What a joy to have the dream come alive once again! But I would have no way of knowing that the road ahead would have many twists and turns that would eventually lead to a very dark place.

I will never forget the first time I saw him. He came to that revival meeting where I was singing, along with his sister, her husband, and their small child. He was very handsome, and all the young girls my age noticed him. They were smitten by his looks and giggled and flirted, doing their best to capture his attention. What I did not know was that his sister fell in love with my singing, my heart, and my spirit. She later told him on their way home from that meeting that he should pursue me because I would make him a great wife. He was a senior in high school and would be graduating in a few months.

Over the next few nights of revival, he returned, along with his sister and her family. I saw all the teenage girls in the church falling over themselves to sit near him, working to gain his attention, and doing anything they could to get his name and phone number. He played the hard-to-get game with them. Unbeknownst to me, his parents were friends with my pastor. His sister told them about me and stated how I would be a great wife and an awesome addition to their family. She pressed them to call my pastor and get my contact information. They called my pastor to find out more. He told them who I was, who my parents were, where I was going to Bible school, and how to get in touch with me.

He called me! Wow, the man that every girl in church wanted to date called me! I could hardly believe my ears. His voice was deep and mature. I was blown away. He asked me if he could come by my house and pick me up to take me to revival. I told him I would ask my dad if it would be okay, asked him for his phone number, and said I would let him know what my dad said. We hung up from that phone call, and I felt like I was floating on air. Dad was in the barn, working, and I remember running up to him and telling him about the phone call, asking his permission to allow this young man to pick me up and drive me to revival. Dad didn't say yes, he didn't say no, but he did say that he needed a few days to make his decision. I was bummed. An opportunity like this does not come along very often, and I did not want this one to slip away.

Dad spoke with our pastor and asked a lot of questions about this young man's family; how long he knew them, their background, etc. He learned that they were of the same legalistic denomination as the Bible school I was attending, they were in full-time evangelistic ministry, and traveled extensively, preaching and singing for many years. After three days, Dad told me it was okay for this handsome young man to escort me to church. Can I just say that I was on cloud nine? I don't even know where cloud nine is, but I was there. The very atmosphere was alive with hope and life! For the first time in a very long time, I felt like I was noticed, special, chosen, desired, and attractive. I remember how nervous I was to make that call to him. A female answered, and I asked if he was there. When I heard his voice on the other end, I felt like I could faint. I gave him the okay to pick me up for revival, gave him directions to my house, set a time to be picked up, and ended the call. I am known to be a patient person, but waiting on the hours to tick by until he came to pick me up was difficult, to say the least. I kept thinking to myself how fortunate I was that he would choose me out of all the available girls in our church.

I went through my closet, trying to decide what to wear. I wanted to look extra special tonight because he was always immaculately dressed. His hair was perfect, and his shoes were so shiny I could see my reflection in them. I threw three different dresses on my bed, trying to decide which one would best match his taste in clothing. Finally, after much deliberating and fussing, I came to the conclusion that I was no nearer a decision than when I started. Leaving the dresses lying on my bed, I went downstairs to give it more thought. I could make a decision after my chores were done.

He arrived early to pick me up, while my family and I were still at the barn, milking the cows. I could not believe he was here early. He saw me in my work clothes, with my hair pulled back in a haphazardly way. I was devastated. I apologized for not being ready yet and informed him that we were finishing up with the milking. This is not how it was supposed to be happening! I informed my parents that he was here to pick me up and told them I had to go. I hurried to the house to get ready while he and his sister and her family waited for me in his car. I dashed to my bedroom, grabbed one of the dresses, and ran to the bathroom where I quickly washed up, brushed my teeth, and combed my hair. No time for any extra prepping! Frazzled and nervous, I walked to the car, and we drove to church.

You can imagine the response of the teenage girls from my church when they saw me getting out of his car! They asked me how I managed to pull this off! They were jealous and let it be known. One of the girls thought she had him all wrapped up, that he was hers, and she told me so. She said that I had stolen him from her, and she was going to steal him away from me, no matter how long it took. That never happened.

I have no recollection what he and I talked about that first evening, but I do remember that he asked if he could pick me up again, to which I responded a quick "Yes!" I was over the moon about him.

We began dating, and he was a bright spot in my day! It didn't matter what the grouchy principal did to me. I had found a new love, and I was not going to allow him to steal my joy. My mind was not on schoolwork. I was conjuring up a way to get out of there, and I saw the possibility at last.

I fell hard and fast for him. I was so immature where relationships are concerned. He was only the third boy that I really cared for, but the first one that I had ever dated, and I was only fifteen years old. Looking back, I see how pathetic we were together. We were both so young and naive. I don't think he knew how to properly treat a girl either. I don't believe that he was ever shown by his dad what godly dating looks like. He never took me to a restaurant, never bought me a present, refused to take me to his graduation to show me off, and only took me to his house to meet his parents one time prior to our marriage. Our dates consisted of him coming to the house, picking me up, and taking me to church or he would come to the house, and we would sit at the kitchen table while I did my homework. Not a great way to start a relationship.

Grade ten finally came to a close, and I vowed that I would never step foot inside that school again! I informed my parents that I was done there, and that my plan was to return to public school. A dreadful thought to once again face the bullying and abuse, but I just knew that I could not remain under the authority of that principal. I was choosing the lesser of two evils, in my opinion. But whatever the outcome, I just knew that I would never return to the Bible school.

You may be thinking by now, why I didn't share any of this with my parents. Well, there are a couple of reasons why I didn't. We were raised to respect our elders and those in authority over us, no matter what. When we started school, we were told that if we got in trouble at school, we would get it twice as hard when we got home. It was the legalist way of thinking. Even though my parents loved us, they did not spare the rod when it came to disciplining us. I am grateful for my upbringing, for it saved me from a lot of things and cultivated in me a godly reverence and respect for God as well as a respect and honor for my parents. So from my earliest experience with bullying in grade one to the nasty principal at the Bible school, I kept it all inside. Another reason I did not share with my parents is that I didn't feel safe in sharing with them. I felt that they would somehow blame me for what was happening. I was so wounded, so hurt, so insecure, and I just couldn't bear the thought that my own parents would turn on me, so I said nothing to them. It was my way of self-protection, choosing rather to stuff my own hurt deep down inside than to expose it and be at risk for getting a tongue-lashing and rejection from my well-meaning disciplinarian parents. They lived by very high standards and expected nothing short of excellence from all of us. There were times when I just felt that I did not measure up.

My dad was a perfectionist. Today, he would be diagnosed with something like obsessive compulsive disorder, but back then, it was just called being extremely particular and perfectionistic. I remember him telling me that if I had done it right the first time, I wouldn't have to do it over again. No matter how hard I tried, it seemed there was always something that was just not right. For all of my childhood, and even into adulthood, I was striving to win their approval and usually fell short. Later in life, I realized that I suffered from the same perfectionism that my dad had, and it nearly destroyed me.

After his graduation from high school, my boyfriend came to see me nearly every night of the week. I welcomed him with open arms. He was my beau, my love, my best and only friend. Even though he did not shower me with kind words of affection or gifts of any kind, I believed, with all my heart, that he loved me as much as I loved him. It would be many painful years before I would learn the raw truth about what he felt for me.

I asked him lots of questions about his family, his sister and her family, and his younger brother who was the same age as my youngest sister. We often talked about his parents and where they were ministering at the time. In addition to pastoring a small church in Lancaster County, Pennsylvania, they traveled all over the US in revivals and camp meetings, preaching and singing. I was ecstatic for them. They were literally living my dream! One evening, he shared with me how he had made a promise to God to be a preacher if his dad got a bear that year in bear hunting season. The morning of bear season, his dad was in the woods, just a short time, and shot and killed a bear. I was so impressed! I thought to myself how blessed I was to have found him! I would fit right in with all of them! I could travel with them, become part of what God was doing through them, and live out the call of God on my life in that way. I couldn't have been more wrong!

The summer between grade ten and eleven was tumultuous in many ways. My boyfriend had just graduated high school and resented the fact that I still had to complete two more years of studies before my own graduation. I asked him if he was going to pursue a Christian education since he had promised God to be a preacher if his dad got a bear, and, sure enough, his dad shot a bear. He told me that he could be a preacher without going to any Bible college. After all, his dad was a preacher and had only gone to grade eight. I informed him that my intention was to graduate high school and then seek continued education somewhere at a reputable Christian college. He was not impressed with that at all. He told me that he didn't approve and that he felt that I was prepared enough for any ministry that God had for me. In fact, I was beginning to get meetings locally where I would serve as worship leader or song evangelist for revivals, youth meetings, special occasions, such as Easter, Mother's Day, etc.

My boyfriend was an avid hunter and trout fisherman, and during trout fishing season in Pennsylvania, he would take every opportunity he could to fish. He was never keen on river or lake fishing, but loved to trout fish. On one occasion, he brought his fishing gear along with him, when he came to see me, and invited me to come along with him. I told him I had a lot of homework, so he told me to bring it along. We went to a small trout stream not far from our farm. He began fishing, and I threw a blanket on the ground and opened my books, preparing to do homework. There was very little conversation between the two of us, and I assumed that he was having a good time fishing. I concentrated on my homework. Suddenly, out of nowhere, he said to me, "I wonder what you would look like with your nose countersunk into your face about three inches!" To say that I was shocked would be an understatement of the year! I asked him where on earth that had come from. What would make him say such a thing.? He came over to where I was sitting, grabbed the book from my hand, and threw it. Papers flew everywhere, and the book landed in a heap.

My homework papers were dirty and torn, and my textbook was all scuffed from landing on the gravel! I was in a state of disbelief. Surely this did not just happen. How could this have happened? Before I could process the event, he reached down and pulled me up to his face. He yelled at me to get my nose out of my books and give him my undivided attention. He told me he was sick and tired of traveling all the way to see me every night, only to have me ignore him while doing homework. I had no idea that he felt this way about my schooling. We had been dating for just a few months. I was over it.

I decided right then and there that I was breaking up with him. I even toyed with the idea of walking home since we were only about a mile from the house. I think he knew that he had just made a big mistake and, switching gears, made the decision to pack up his fishing stuff, and take me back home. I had every intention of giving him his walking papers, so to speak, because he had shown me a side of him that I had not seen before and never wanted to see again.

By the time we reached my home, I had prepared the short speech that would end our relationship. But he had his own speech ready. When we pulled up in front of my home, he reached over and took my hand. He began to apologize to me for his actions down by the creek. He then proceeded to tell me that I was ready to be his wife, that he needed me to be his wife, and that he was not leaving there until I promised to be his wife. He was so convincing, so assuring, so persuasive that I fell for it. From that moment, we began to plan how to get me out of school so we could be married. We talked about eloping, but I told him that I was underage, and my parents could have the wedding annulled. We talked about running away to another part of the country and getting married. Neither of those things happened, and one day led to another.

Before we knew it, summer was past, and the time came for me to begin my junior year in high school. I had informed my parents that I would not be returning to the private Bible school, and if they insisted, I would run away, and they would never see me again. I knew I had a plan to back that up because my boyfriend and I had already talked about that possibility. The evening before my junior year began, my boyfriend asked me if I was going to school the next day. I said that I was, and he became angry. He called me names like "sissy" and "little school girl." I was hurt and angry myself. After all, I felt that I was doing the best that I could under the circumstances, and that he was being unreasonable.

Grade eleven was a bit of a blur. I was there in body, but my thoughts were far from school. In my mind, I was married and very involved in full-time ministry. I envisioned our life together as we traveled in ministry, singing, speaking, preaching, and living out the dream. It couldn't happen soon enough! The Bible says that hope deferred makes the heart sick (Proverbs 13:12). My heart was definitely sick from waiting and longing to fulfill my destiny. I just had to figure out a way to make it a reality.

Hindsight is twenty-twenty, but in the thick of things, living it out, one moment at a time, one cannot always see the forest for the trees. So it was with me. I didn't have spiritual insight. I lacked spiritual maturity, and I failed to seek God for His divine will in my life, regarding the man that I should marry. I realized, many years later, that Satan had used my boyfriend as bait in a trap that would ensnare me, hold me hostage, rob me of my joy in serving the Lord, kill my dream of being a teacher/missionary, and steal my God-given destiny.

CHAPTER 4

Caught in the Trap

OUR RELATIONSHIP WAS ROCKY, BUT I WAS determined to make it work. He was not happy with me being in school. I was sidetracked, and my grades were slipping, and all he wanted was for me to quit school and marry him. Christmas that year was a turning point for me. He told me that the only thing he would accept from me for Christmas was for me to quit school and marry him. I decided that it was time to clue my parents in on our plan. I was scared to bring the topic up with them face-to-face, so I decided it might be best to write them a letter. I sat down and, in the best way I knew, expressed my desire to leave school, marry my boyfriend, join with his family in ministry, and get on with the rest of my life, living out my calling, walking out my dream. I put the letter in an envelope and left it on their bed. Needless to say, my parents were not impressed. My mom was the first one to read it. Her response was one of yelling, throwing the letter in my face, and asking me what in the world was going on between my ears. I tried to explain, but her immense disapproval nearly shut me down. I found it difficult to even speak to her. I could not look her in the eyes. All I ever wanted was her approval, but in that moment, I felt humiliation and regret. She expressed her intense shame of me for writing such a ridiculous letter and told me to just wait until my dad read it, then I would get what was coming to me.

Dad read the letter and called me to come and have a seat. He reacted in a more civil manner to the letter than my mom had, and he wanted to know more details about what had prompted me to write it. His unexpected tenderness brought me to tears, and I poured out my heart to him. I explained how I felt that God had brought my boyfriend into my life. I talked to Dad about the various conversations my boyfriend and I had regarding me joining up with his parents in ministry, and how it just made sense to me to get married sooner than later. He listened to me with an intensity that I had not witnessed before. Mom stood nearby, and even though I did not look at her, I felt her eyes burning a hole in my heart. She did not speak, but her presence was screaming at me. After I finished speaking, Dad simply said that I needed to finish school, no ifs, ands, or buts about it. And Mom had to get her two cents in by yelling that the only way I would marry that boy would be over her dead body!

As I take time to reflect back on those years, and what I put them through, I cannot blame my poor parents for the way they acted and reacted to my antics. I was not using common sense, for sure, nor was I seeking godly wisdom or counsel, and had been completely taken in by the enemy's bait. Only I never realized it until much, much later in life.

When I shared with my boyfriend about the letter and what had transpired, he was upset. Over the next little while, his strategy changed. Instead of being content to sit at the table while I worked on homework, he wanted to go for a drive or take a walk. He began pressing me to be intimate! He reasoned it out by telling me that I was already his wife in my heart, already committed to this relationship, so it was okay. God knew our intention to be married. It was just a matter of a piece of paper, just a formality. I knew it was wrong! I knew what the Bible said, and I knew my parents trusted me to live up to my profession. But let me tell you, in a moment of weakness, and acting out of fear of losing him, I caved. I couldn't believe I had allowed this to happen. I had failed God, and my heart was broken. I felt the sting of shame when I read His Word, and when I prayed, the fervor was gone, and the words seemed to float right above my head for a few seconds, then fall to the floor and shatter like fragile glass, into a million broken pieces. We continued to seek opportunity to act like a married couple, and the weight of that disobedience weighed heavily on my heart.

Oh, how I longed to return to a place of purity, how I regretted my decision to lower my standard! The depth of shame I felt when I sat at the piano and played a hymn and sang out to the Lord nearly crushed me. I knew that I had broken God's heart, and here I was, making a feeble attempt to continue on as though the sin had never happened. No matter how much I longed to return to that place of purity and innocence, it was impossible to do, for that place no longer existed. My innocence had been stolen. I lived in a new reality, and I did not like it.

The enemy of our soul is cunning, and we are fooling ourselves if we believe that we can outsmart him. He knows our areas of strength, and he knows where we are weak. He knows when to attack, how to attack, and what weapon will do the most damage. He set the trap with the bait that he knew I would not be able to resist. And once I took the bait, all I wanted was more! There is pleasure in sin for a season, but, oh, the devastation that lingers long after the fun has faded!

Valentine's Day was approaching, and he wanted to be married on that day. I had to get creative quickly or I might lose him forever. Suddenly, I knew what I must do, and I put the plan into action. After eating breakfast, I would go into the bathroom and pretend to be sick, making noise like I was throwing up. I had to convince my mom that I was sick so I could stay home from school. It took some convincing. She would take my temperature, which was always normal, and tell me to get to school. This went on for several days. One morning, after I had gone through my routine of pretending to be sick, Mom asked me if I was pregnant. I told her that I could be. She grabbed hold of me and shook me by my shoulders and said, "Well, you had better not be. That's all I've got to say!"

Even though I was upset by how she acted toward me, I had a sense of accomplishment that my plan might actually be working. I went to school that day to avoid her cold stares, knowing that I was the source of her pain.

When I returned home from school, Mom informed me that I had to go into the bathroom and give a urine sample for the doctor. After I left that morning, she had contacted the doctor. She was told that a urine sample could be collected at home as long as she had a sterile container to collect it in. Mom went to the doctor's office and picked up a sterile container and placed it in our bathroom. I was taken aback. She had acted so quickly on this. Now, it had become real! It was no longer just a plan in my head. It was playing out before my very eyes. Fooling my parents was one thing, but attempting to get a false positive reading on a pregnancy test was a whole different matter!

You might be asking right now, "Why were you so eager to quit school and get married?" I will tell you why. I believed that school was hindering me from walking out my God-given calling. I truly believed with all my being that God had placed this handsome young man in my life. He was the springboard that would catapult me into the position I needed to get to in ministry. School was a huge boulder on my pathway that was hindering me from realizing my full potential in God! My desire to be in ministry was consuming me. It is all I ever thought about!

And, suddenly, this man drops into my life. He looks good, sounds good, his parents are living my dream, and they are willing to take me into their ministry. It had to be a God thing! It just had to be! And I felt an overwhelming sense of urgency! I had to make it happen now! Looking back, I see how the enemy planted his snake eggs in my head, and those eggs hatched into what became thoughts that found a lodging place in my mind. Those thoughts were driving my actions, and I did not realize it. I never sat down and thought it through. I never considered the impact my actions would have. Once I took the enemy's bait, all other options, in my mind, were off the table. I had to follow through with the plan. I loved God and my parents and did not want to disappoint them, but I also loved my boyfriend. Life was complicated.

As I prepared to give a urine sample, my mind was reeling at how I was going to produce a positive pregnancy test from my urine. I knew I was not pregnant! Desperation set in. What could I do? How could I pull this off? In a linen closet in the bathroom, I found a small bottle of nail polish remover. After peeing in the small cup, I took that bottle of nail polish remover, opened the lid, and put a few drops of that liquid into my urine sample. I had no idea if it would work, but I was at a point in my life where I was willing to take the chance! I closed the lid, washed my hands, put the nail polish remover back, walked out of the restroom, and handed the cup to Mom who was waiting by the bathroom door. She took it from me without saying a word, but her expression spoke volumes. Her face told me that she was ashamed of me to the core of her being.

She took the urine sample to the doctor's office where she was told that we would know the results in a few days. I was holding on to hope that I had somehow managed to pull off something nearly impossible—faking a pregnancy test! In that moment, I had resolved in my heart that no matter the outcome of that test, I was going to quit school, marry my man, and move into the ministry God was calling me to.

When the call came in, we were getting ready to eat lunch. Mom had made some soup, and I was hungry. The phone rang, and she picked it up and said hello. After a few seconds, her face went white. She looked like she was going to be sick, and she hung up the phone. She had a box of crackers in her hand, and she threw them across the kitchen table. The box flew open, and the crackers went all over the floor as she screamed, "Well, they got the test results, and it's not good! The rabbit died!"

The rabbit died! This was the result I was hoping for! Years ago, laboratory rabbits were used to determine a pregnancy. If the rabbit died, the test was positive for pregnancy. My mom had just been told that the rabbit died, and I was pregnant. Only thing was, I was not pregnant at all. Only God and I knew at that moment what the real truth was.

Even though I was upset to see Mom so distraught, inside, I was rejoicing that my plan had actually worked! It didn't matter that I was not really pregnant. I had managed to fool a test into a false reading. I could hardly wait to tell my boyfriend the great news!

After that phone call from the doctor confirming a positive pregnancy test, tension reigned supreme in our home. There was an air of disappointment that hung over every conversation. Laughter was nonexistent, and I felt a heavy weight of responsibility and shame for causing such a mess.

The next few weeks were tense, and conversation had nearly ground to a halt. Short sentences took the place of lengthy dialogue between my parents. My sisters were distant and cold, and my one sister told my mom that I had no idea what I was in for. She meant the giving birth part, but she was so right on target. I had no idea what I was in for. Lord, help me, Jesus! There is so much truth to this statement: "What a tangled web we weave when we set out to deceive!" It was never my intention to deceive anyone. It was never my intention to disappoint my Lord Jesus or my parents. It was never my intention to bring dishonor to the name of Jesus Christ, and, yet, I had managed to do just that! I had let so many people down. My actions brought shame to our entire family. I had a lot of repenting to do, and I sought the Lord earnestly in my shame and disgrace! I pleaded with Him for forgiveness! Even though I believed that God had forgiven me, it would be many, many years before I would forgive myself!

We were married on March 2, 1974, in a small ceremony officiated by my pastor and my husband's dad. After the wedding, we had a small reception for a few folks at our farmhouse. I tried to be the exuberant bride, but a heaviness hung over the day like a dark cloud, and, in my heart, I knew that this was not right. Something was just not right. Nevertheless, we had exchanged vows before God and witnesses, and we were married. As we proclaimed our love for each other, promising to love and cherish one another till death us do part, the trap snapped shut! I had no way of knowing on my wedding day that the pain of being in that trap would usher me into a very dark place that would require more faith in my God than I ever dreamed possible! I would face situations that would challenge me on every level—spiritually, financially, physically, relationally, psychologically, and geographically! The trap had snapped! The effects of that trap snapping shut rippled down through the years of time, leaving a trail of tears, heartache, betrayal, and death in its wake.

CHAPTER 5

The Rude Awakening

OUR WEDDING DAY WAS A COLD, BLUSTERY, snowy Saturday in March. I was two months shy of my seventeenth birthday. We did not go on a honeymoon. I was okay with that because I knew that we would be joining his family on a vacation later on that summer. We left my parents' home after the wedding reception and followed my husband's parents to Lancaster County where they pastored a small country church. They wanted to introduce us to their congregation the next day. However, plans changed, and we did not spend our wedding night there but instead drove back to his parents' home. This is where we would live until we could find a place of our own. Their property is in a narrow, long valley nestled between two mountain ranges in Central Pennsylvania. The population is sparse. The homes are scattered along the twisting, winding road that leads through the valley, and the nearest town is about twelve miles away. Wild game is prevalent with an abundance of black bears, deer, and turkeys.

Their home was a small bungalow with two bedrooms and one bathroom. The bedroom that we slept in had been shared by my husband and his younger brother. When we got married, his brother agreed to sleep on the couch in the living room, allowing us to have our privacy. It was not an ideal way to begin our marriage, but we were not thinking about that at all. We were all consumed with our own selves and paid no mind to our loved ones who were feeling the negative impact of our selfishness.

On Monday, March 4, two days after our wedding, I was standing at the stove, preparing breakfast for my new husband. His mother walked up to me and said, "Let's get something straight. My son will always love me more than he loves you! I am his mother, and I will always be his mother!"

I had never had the privilege of knowing his parents. I knew of them but had never built a relationship with them, and here we were, under the same roof, each of us desperately needing our own privacy, and yet not finding it. To hear the words from his mom that morning was mind-boggling. At first, I could not even comprehend what she was trying to say. I stood there, staring at her in disbelief, trying to determine whether she was serious or joking. She turned away in a huff, and I realized the seriousness of her statement! After the shock wore off, and I was able to mentally regroup, I got angry. I thought to myself, *Well, I'll show you! I am young and sexy, and he is married to me. He is going to bed with me! I will prove to you that you are wrong!* But she was absolutely correct! Time would prove her right, over and over and over again.

I had another thing on my mind that day of utmost importance. I had to figure out a way to act pregnant. That is a monumental task to pull off. Let me tell you. I practiced pushing my stomach out in a little bulge to make it look like I might be starting to get a baby bump, but I didn't manage that too well. Sometimes, I would forget about it, and my belly would be flat. My mother-in-law noticed and commented on how strange it was that some days, I looked pregnant, and some days, I didn't. I knew I had to up my game, but what was I to do?

When my mother-in-law made that statement two days after our wedding, my husband and father-in-law heard her say it. Neither one of them corrected her. I could not believe what I was witnessing. That same night, after we had gone to bed and been intimate, my husband suddenly got out of bed and left the bedroom. I thought he was going to the restroom, but he was gone for a long time. When he did not return, I tiptoed to our bedroom door, opened it quietly, and peered into the hallway. The house was dark and quiet. The door to my in-laws' bedroom was closed. I stood there, staring at the door, wondering where my husband had gone. Finally, I got up the courage to knock on their door. His dad came to the door and asked me what I wanted. I said I was looking for my husband.

At that point, his mom turned on the bedroom light and there, in the middle of the bed was my husband, laying between his mom and dad. A wave of disbelief swept over me, and I felt like I was going to be sick. I asked him if he was okay, and he said he was fine. I asked him what he was doing, and he said he was sleeping. Confused, hurt, feeling all kinds of messed up, I went back to our bedroom and closed the door. I did not sleep much that night. It was just the beginning of a very long journey of pain, rejection, and abuse that would end in a near tragedy.

Night after night, the same routine was repeated. After acting like two married people in the privacy of our bedroom, my husband would go to his parents' bed and sleep in the middle, between them. Morning after morning, we would gather in the kitchen for breakfast, and conversation would be about the weather, news, world events, anything but what was going on in the house. It was wearing on me mentally. I thought to myself, *Either I am crazy or this family is crazy! What in the world is wrong with this picture?*

My husband's rejection felt like someone punched me in the gut! To make matters worse, his mom paraded around the house in triumph, while I sank into a state of confusion and depression. I had gone to great lengths to fool everyone, had convinced my parents to allow me to quit school and marry this man, and had big dreams and high hopes of walking in obedience to God in ministry. And now he wasn't even sleeping with me in our bed! None of this made any sense.

Then, horror of horrors, ten days into our marriage, I got my period! Oh no! I hid in the bathroom for a very long time, not wanting the truth to be discovered. I had two options as I saw things: I could tell everyone the truth and eat humble pie or I could say that my pregnancy was in trouble, and I was bleeding. I chose the second option. I called my mother-in-law into the bathroom and showed her the blood in the toilet. She gasped and asked me if I wanted to go to the hospital. I told her no and said I just wished to lie down and rest. Everyone was very concerned about the pregnancy, and I felt guilty over the attention I was getting. I was experiencing some cramping that is normal with a period, but I exaggerated it a bit and spent a lot of time hanging out in the bathroom, trying to come up with plan B of the big lie. I made the decision to fake a miscarriage. Yep, that would be the easiest route to go at this point in the game. My husband was not sleeping with me anyway, so what did I have to lose?

I hardly saw him for the next three days and spent a lot of time in our bedroom, contemplating the mess I found myself in. I thought how in the world did this get so messed up? It was a Friday morning, just thirteen days into our marriage. Things were very rocky between us. Tension in the house was thick, and I distanced myself from everyone. Right around the time that I would be going to the kitchen to join the family for breakfast, there was a knock on the bedroom door. I walked to the door and opened it. My mother-in-law stood there, looking serious and stern. She told me that they were getting company that day, and she did not want me to come out of the bedroom at all. She told me that my moodiness would ruin the visit, and she did not want her guests to even know that I was in the house. She said, "We don't want to see you or hear you. Is that clear?"

With that, she turned and walked away. My husband had left for the day and gone to work without even saying goodbye to me. I slowly closed the bedroom door, stumbled to the bed, and collapsed in a heap. Overtaken in grief and disbelief, I sobbed and cried, buried my face in the pillows to stifle the sounds. I suddenly missed my parents beyond words. Homesickness overwhelmed me. I had not spoken to them since my wedding day and had never been away from them this long before. I missed my sisters, I missed my dog, I missed everything about the farm. I even missed the routine of getting up at four every morning.

I stayed in the bedroom for the entire day while my in-laws visited with their guests, eating, laughing, and talking for hours. Just on the other side of the wall, I could hear everything that was happening. I didn't go to the bathroom, didn't get a drink, didn't have anything to eat. Here is what I did do: I packed my clothes into the clothes hamper that my mom had given me for my sixteenth birthday, just ten months prior. I had made up my mind that I was mistreated for the last time. I knew that this would be the last day I spent in that house.

By the time my husband got home from work, the visitors had gone. It took a while for him to come to the bedroom, and when he did, I was ready for him. I told him that I was sick of being treated so poorly, how I was made to stay in the bedroom for the entire day, not having anything to eat or drink, not allowed to even use the toilet. I told him I wanted to go home. He said, "Let's go!"

I walked over and picked up the clothes hamper that held all my belongings on this earth and walked out of the house. His parents were on the carport and asked what was up. My husband told them that I wanted to go home. My mother-in-law made a smart remark about me going to get some titty! Everybody laughed. I put the hamper in the back seat of our car, got in, and shut the door.

We rode in silence most of the way because my husband had the radio blaring. At one point, I reached over to turn the volume down so I could talk, but he shoved my hand away and turned the volume up even louder. So there was no sense in trying to have a conversation.

When we pulled up at the front of our farmhouse, my mom came to the front door. The look on her face said she was very anxious to see us. She came running down the sidewalk to greet us. I had started to open the door to exit the car when, suddenly, my husband took his foot and kicked me out, onto the ground. I flew out fast and landed hard. My mom gasped, and I jumped up quickly. Mom said, "What on earth is going on?"

My husband looked at her and said, "You can have her back. We don't want her!" It took a while for that to really sink in. He didn't say, "I don't want her." He said, "We don't want her!"

Just as he said those words, he reached in the back seat, took my hamper, and threw it. The lid flew open, and the contents spilled out onto the front yard. My mom was in shock! My husband jumped into his car, floored it, and spun out down the road. I stood at the end of the sidewalk. My mom was halfway between the house and where I was standing, and my clothes were scattered like rags on the lawn.

CHAPTER 6

What Now?

THIRTEEN DAYS. OUR MARRIAGE HAD LASTED JUST thirteen days. But they were not short days. They were long and painful, filled with betrayal, rejection, bullying, name-calling, alienation, isolation, and mental torture. Mom and I stood and watched my new husband drive down the road and disappear. I drew in a deep breath, and my eyes met her gaze. She looked like a deer caught in the headlights. Disbelief was written all over her face. What had just happened? I had lived out the last thirteen days, had experienced the brutal reality firsthand, but Mom did not have a clue. I was not given any way to contact my parents, so once I left them on my wedding day, there was no communication between me and them. Suddenly, without warning, I am standing at the end of their sidewalk, and my belongings have been thrown from the car like discarded trash. So many unanswered questions that day would remain unanswered for years and years.

I ran toward Mom with my arms extended, she reached out and grabbed me, pulling me into her embrace, and I sobbed. She didn't say anything for the longest time, just held me and let me cry. No words were necessary. We were both speaking to each other through an unwritten and unspoken language, the language of love.

When I was somewhat composed, I walked to where my clothes, like strewn debris, in so many ways, reflected the condition of my emotions: ragged, wounded, damaged.

Mom helped me gather my things and put them inside the clothes hamper, and we went inside the house. As soon as we were inside, she looked at me and said, "Are you pregnant?"

I answered, "No."

She said, "I knew it."

No more pretense, no more hiding, no more lies! The truth was out.

Two months had gone by without a word from my husband. I had not made any attempt to contact him either. I was confused, hurt, and at a loss to understand how things had gone from bliss to bust so quickly. My seventeenth birthday was in a few days, and I had held on to hope that he would remember it and come to see me or at least call. Nothing. No visit, no call, no card. It was as if I did not even exist.

I found a job at a local nursing home, working in the kitchen as a dishwasher. It was not the ideal job, but it gave me a bit of spending money. This separation would be only the first of many throughout the course of our turbulent marriage, and God would show up countless times to rescue me. I needed to just hang on to Him. Oh, how I needed to hang on to HIM.

I bought a car. It was an ugly big old boat of a car, an old Chevy Impala. It was burgundy in color with faded paint, foul smelling cloth seats, and looked like something that my Pap would drive. But it was a set of wheels, and it was mine. It was way better than walking. I think I paid $500 for it. I had to borrow the money for it from the bank, so I had a car payment for the first time in my life. Working as a dishwasher proved to be hard work with little pay, but it allowed me to pay that car off early. That car would serve me well for some time, for which I am grateful.

Six months had passed since our wedding, and one evening, Dad announced that he had enough of the nonsense, and he was going to seek an attorney and have the wedding annulled. After all, there had been no contact whatsoever from my husband nor had I made an attempt to contact him. Why would I? He had literally kicked me out of the car, onto the road, and told Mom that they did not want me anymore. I do not need to be told twice where I am welcome and where I am not. The question that loomed large in my head was WHY?

I remember going to my bedroom that evening, following Dad's announcement about his plans to end the sham of a marriage. In my heart, my marriage was real, it was genuine, and I took my marriage vows seriously. I was troubled in my spirit and had to seek the face of Jesus. I cried out to God and asked Him to show me what to do. The answer I received back was, "Your husband has the right to know. It is his marriage too." I shook my head in agreement as if to show God that I understood the message loudly and clearly. I knew what I had to do. I placed the call and asked to speak to my husband. When his voice came on the other end, our conversation was brief. I simply stated that it had been six months without a single word from him, which indicated a total disregard for our marriage and for me as an individual. I told him that if he wanted to be married to me, he had to show up or the wedding would be annulled. The phone call was under two minutes in length. I hung up and breathed a prayer, letting God know that I had done what He asked me to do, and now the rest was up to Him.

Within an hour, my husband and his dad were at our front door. Both of our dads were upset, each with their own reason and wanting to protect their respective offspring. His dad said my dad had no right to annul the wedding because he had married us and "what God has put together, let not man put asunder."

My dad said, "This is no marriage. It's a joke! And I am ending it because of how he has treated my daughter," pointing to my husband who stood in our kitchen, not saying a word.

Dad began to throw a lot of questions at my husband, like why did he insist on me quitting school to marry him, only to have him kick me out of the car, just thirteen days after our wedding day, and then act like I didn't exist by totally ignoring me for six months? Dad tried every way he knew to get answers out of my husband, to no avail. He would not say a word.

Tempers flared, and a scuffle erupted between the two dads. My husband ran out the front door. He ran down the road and never looked back. He told me later that he had feared for his life. I assured him that my dad was frustrated because he was looking for some answers, and my husband refused to speak with him or answer any of his questions.

Dad never did seek counsel about having the wedding annulled, but it put a bit of fire under my husband's butt, and we started to date again.

After three months, he asked me to move back to his house. My answer was firm. No. I would not move back into his parents' house. I told him it was time for us to get our own place, perhaps a small apartment, close to where he worked. He told me that he had no intention of ever leaving his parents' home, so I said that we were at a dead end.

Eventually, he agreed to look at an apartment in town, close to his place of employment. On the day that we were to look at the apartment, I drove from my parents' house to his parents' house where we would both ride together to check out our first home as a married couple. I was excited and hopeful. When I got to his parents' house, I was told that we would all be going to see the apartment. I didn't understand what he meant by that, but quickly, it became real. His parents came out of their house; his sister, her husband, and small child came out of their house that was behind the in-law's house on the same property; and my husband's younger brother came out of the house—eight of us in total.

I shook my head in disbelief as we began piling into two vehicles to go check out an apartment. And to make matters worse, I was told that I would be riding in the back of the car as his parents would be riding with him in the front seat. My first impulse was to protest, but then I thought better of it and slumped into the back seat, alongside his younger brother. His sister, her husband, and their young son followed after us.

The apartment was on the second floor. It was plain but nicely painted, consisted of two bedrooms, a kitchen, living room, and a bath. I found it completely doable and imagined how I could turn that space into our first home. His mom quickly shot it down, even before we got inside the building. She said we would get tired of the stairs. There was no off-street parking, and the noise of traffic would keep us from sleeping. Once inside, she tore apart everything from the color of the walls to the bare, hardwood floors. At the end of the tour, she was the one who made the decision that we would not be renting that apartment. I was furious. I kept thinking, *What in the world is this to her? Why is she permitted to make this kind of decision about where we are going to live?*

I attempted to pull my husband aside to ask him what his thoughts were, but she stuck to him like glue, and the two of them were inseparable. The owner of the apartment building was kind and gracious, giving us our space. After just a brief tour of the apartment, my mother-in-law told the owner that this would not suit, and we would not be renting from her. I could not believe what I was hearing. My husband did not have a word to say. His mom had done all the talking. WHY?

I drove back to my parents' house in a troubled state of mind. What now, God? Where do we go from here?

A couple of days later, my husband called me to tell me that he was going to look at a mobile home sales lot to see what was available for sale. His parents had agreed to allow him to move a mobile home onto their property a little off to the side and slightly behind their house. I told him that sounded good and agreed to meet him there at the sales lot.

Wouldn't you know that he had a car full? Yep, his parents in the front seat, and his sister and her family in the back seat. I was not surprised, but I was disgusted. Could we not make this decision on our own? Did his whole family have to be involved in every area of our lives? I was over it, but they were not going away, so guess who had to give in? You guessed it, yours truly.

After going into several mobile homes, I had my heart set on one that I thought would serve us well as our first home. But his mom had a different opinion altogether. She ended up choosing the mobile home that I would be living in for the next twelve years! It was tiny, twelve-by-forty-five-feet. I hated everything about it, but mostly I hated it because she picked it. She was not paying for it. We were. She kept saying, "This is good enough for you."

To this day, I cannot stand those words!

We purchased that mobile home, and it was moved into place on his parents' land. A new beginning in our marriage began to take shape.

We had a roof over our heads, we had electricity, but we had no running water. I had to carry water from a small stream on their property, boil the water on the gas stove to use for drinking and cooking.

Water was carried for bathing and laundry. We used an outhouse, which was located far from our house, up in the woods behind his sister's trailer. It was not easy by any means. We lived like that for over two years. In the winter, I broke the ice with a pickax and carried the ice in a bucket to our trailer. I was in training but did not realize it at the time. God was preparing me for what lay ahead. My grandparents sold me their wringer washing machine, and I put it on a wooden platform that I built outside our back door. I had no clothes dryer, so everything had to be hung outside on a clothesline.

In the winter, my hands would freeze fast to the clothes that had blown stiff before I could even get the clothespins in place. I was unwillingly enrolled in God's school of learning. His lessons were hard to swallow, but they would prove necessary for me to be able to move into my next assignment.

I asked my husband if we could have a phone in our house. He said he would ask his parents. They denied my request, stating that they had a phone in their garden shed/workshop. I could use that in the event of an emergency. Other than that, the only way of communication was through the postal service. So mailing letters became the normal way of life for me.

As time wore on, I was more and more isolated from the world around me. I was forbidden to have friends, had no phone, was not permitted to take the car to go anywhere, and pretty much stayed within the parameter of their property. I was a prisoner being held in a cell with no visible bars. It was in that environment that I would be stripped of my identity, my self-worth, my joy, my hope, my voice. I was in a loveless marriage where mental abuse happened every day. The name-calling, the belittling, the ongoing rejection as he continued to go to his parents' bed to sleep between them. Our marriage was dysfunctional in every way possible. There was no communication between us, except when he wanted me to do my duty as his wife.

After that, the name-calling would resume. Some of his frequent names he called me were frog eyes, wart lips, wet dog, and hog breath. He would often tell me to go ride my broom. He and his family members would sit on their carport and make mooing sounds when they saw me outside. And I was very thin back then. We had always attended church regularly. I served as church pianist, youth director, stand-in speaker when our pastor was away, Sunday school secretary, worship leader, Sunday school teacher. My husband and I frequently sang as a couple in our church. In spite of the fact that we looked pretty good from the outside, we were anything but good on the inside. Abuse reigned supreme, and I struggled every day from the effects that were only visible inside my heart. My mind was in turmoil. I knew something was wrong, but I couldn't put my finger on what it was. Well, in time, I would find out.

CHAPTER 7

The Diagnosis

I REMEMBER THAT DAY AS IF IT were yesterday. We had been married not quite two years. He was standing in our tiny kitchen, and I was in our living room. He had his hand under his nose, palm down, and was gently puffing air from his nose, onto the back of his hand in short, quick bursts. I stood there and watched him, not sure of what I was looking at. This behavior went on for some time. He seemed to be unaware that I was even watching him. Finally, I spoke up and asked my husband what he was doing. He told me that he was checking to see if he was still breathing. I had no idea how to even process that. I have a reputation of being quick-witted, and before I could even think about what I was saying, these words came flying out into the atmosphere, "Well, if you stop breathing, you will be the first person to know it, and I will be the second." I had no way of knowing that my husband was on a journey that would take him into the world of mental illness. I, along with our daughter, would get pulled into the abyss with him, and we would have to hang on for our very lives.

The symptoms had actually started to present just eighteen months into our marriage. He began to miss a lot of work, saying that he did not feel like going to work. When I questioned whether he was sick, he would tell me no, but then he would say that he couldn't go to work. During those eighteen months, we had been separated three times, with me moving back home for a bit. These separations were hard on every member on both sides of our family. My parents were sick and tired of me showing up, now and again, and disrupting their home. My two younger sisters were still in school, and each time I separated from my husband, it sent them on their own emotional roller-coaster ride. I was so caught up in my own pain that I failed to even notice what my decisions were doing to my family. Truth be known, I would hang in as long as I could, take the abuse until I couldn't, and when I felt like I was going to die if I stayed one more minute longer, I would jump in my car and head to my parents' house for a few weeks.

My husband's boss called his parents' house since we had no phone in our house. He asked my husband if the three of us could meet him at a cabin that he had in the mountains, located an hour from where we lived. We drove there to meet up with him. He expressed to both of us that unless my husband improved his attendance at work, he would probably be let go. This man really liked my husband and had trained him personally. He was looking for answers as to what was happening that caused him to miss so much work. I had no answers, and my husband refused to talk about what he was dealing with. We left the cabin that night, and my husband's employment with that company would soon come to an abrupt end. I thought it would just be a matter of time before he would find work somewhere else, but he never worked again.

Then the panic attacks began. He said it felt like he was having a heart attack. We hurried twenty-two miles to the emergency room where a multitude of tests were performed, all inconclusive. We would drive back home with no answers, only to have it happen again. Months went by, and the panic attacks were increasing in frequency, duration, and severity. Many trips to the emergency room would result in the same outcome—inconclusive. I asked the doctor if my husband could be admitted for observation and was told that would not be permitted. When pressed, he told me that my husband was no threat to himself or to others. That was about to change.

It was a cold winter evening, the snow was deep, and the temperature was frigid. My husband had been in bed for three days, only getting up to go over to his parents' house for a while. They had just left for the weekend to travel to their church in Lancaster County and would not be back home for a couple of days. I was in the living room, reading, when he came out of the bedroom and opened the back door. I looked up in time to see him going out into the bitter cold with nothing on. I mean, he was completely naked. In his hand, he had a belt. I hurried after him, asking him what he was doing. He did not answer me, and he had gotten a good head start, so he kept going into the woods behind our house. I followed through the knee-deep snow, struggling to catch up to him. It was cold, I had no shoes on, did not take time to grab a coat, and I knew he had to be nearly frozen because he was wearing nothing at all. He had been born here, knew the area like the back of his hand, and knew exactly where he was headed. His goal was a huge tree with large, low limbs that he could easily reach from the ground. He got to that tree and attempted to end his life with his belt around one of those limbs.

I struggled with him to get the belt out of his hands, all the while assuring him that I was going to get him help, but he had to come back to the house with me. He refused to go. He said he had to end his life because the voices were telling him to. I knew I had to get him to the hospital ASAP. I literally dragged him back to our little trailer, got him inside, and managed to get him dressed. His eyes were wild. He was not able to focus, and I was frightened beyond words. We had been in the frigid cold for twenty minutes. My feet were nearly frozen, and his body was purplish and cold. I prayed and asked God for guidance and informed him that he was going to the hospital. He didn't say anything but refused to move. I pulled and tugged and pulled and pleaded with him to please move his feet. After what seemed like a lifetime, I managed to get him outside, lead him to the car, and get him inside. He went nearly unresponsive as I drove to the hospital, twenty-two miles away. We had made that trip so often in the past, but this time, there was a heightened sense of urgency.

We arrived at the ER where he refused to get out of the car and go inside the hospital. No amount of pleading made any difference. He would not listen to reason and said he was not going into that hospital under any circumstances. I took the keys, exited the car, and told him to wait right there for me, and that I would be back. I hurried inside the ER and told the first person I met that I had an emergency. My husband needed to be seen. I relayed to them what had taken place in the woods. I was told that the only way they could treat my husband was if he would walk through the doors on his own. They were not legally permitted to go outside of the doors to get him. I took a wheelchair with me and hurried to the car. I told him that these people were here to help him and tried to pull him out of the car, into the wheelchair. He would not budge.

I returned the wheelchair to the hospital and begged the nurse to please come outside and help convince him to come in and be seen. She refused, saying it was not legal. He had to walk in on his own or be pushed inside in a wheelchair. I told her that I was not going anywhere because if I took him home in the state of mind he was in, someone in our house was going to die. I said, "If you can't admit him, then admit me. Because I can't take it anymore."

She said there was no reason to admit me. I returned to the car. This time, by the grace of God, he agreed to come with me inside the hospital. They were waiting just inside the doors, and when we walked through the first set of double doors, they grabbed him and hoisted him onto a stretcher and hurried him down a long hallway. I nearly collapsed. My legs went limp, my brain felt numb, and I was trembling uncontrollably. I don't remember too much of what happened after they whisked him away that night. He was admitted to the psychiatric unit and was there for several months. I was not able to visit him that night because it was after visiting hours, so I returned the next day. When I saw him, he was laying on a bare mattress on the floor, in a room without windows. I was not permitted to enter the room. I could only observe him from a tiny window in the huge reinforced steel door. He had no clothes on. He was laying very still and did not respond to my voice. I had no idea what was going on and asked if he had eaten or gone to the bathroom.

I was told that he had done none of those things. He was offered water but refused. He was offered something to eat but stared off in the distance as if in a trance. He would be like this for many days. I later learned that he had a total nervous collapse or breakdown. The road to recovery would be long, arduous, and painful.

After he was diagnosed with paranoid schizophrenia, the medicine trial-and-error journey began. Many different combinations were tried, all with their own set of side effects, until the right mix was found to work.

Eventually, he was good enough to return home. I rarely saw him, except on the weekends when his parents traveled to their church. He spent most of his time either at their house or at his sister's trailer right behind us.

I had my own battles with the mind. The enemy was doing a good job of feeding me lies, and I was falling for his shenanigans. I had lost sight of my self-worth, the constant name-calling had worn away my confidence in who I was and whose I was, and the dream I had of walking in my calling in ministry seemed to be light-years in the past, hidden away where only God could see. That dream was dead and gone. I was just a shell of the person God had called me to be. I never smiled, never laughed, never enjoyed life. But then something happened that changed everything. It was a beautiful spring day, and I took my Bible and walked into the woods behind our house to find a comfortable place to read God's Word. I found a big log on the forest floor that had long ago been a majestic tree. Years of time had come and gone until all that remained was this big log that was covered in moss. I sat down and opened my Bible and began to read. God met me there. I felt His presence for the first time in a long time, and hope began to be reborn. I felt God's presence so real there that I didn't want to leave. I looked around, and all was peaceful there in the woods that day.

I made a promise to myself that I would come back here to this spot again. And I did. I made that log my altar, the place where I went on a daily basis to meet up with God. I learned so much there. It was here where God would show up in a mighty way and give me the strength to press on for the journey ahead.

CHAPTER 8

The Car

WE WERE SEPARATED AGAIN, AND I WAS once again living at home with my parents. I was riding with my dad to town when I noticed it! A gorgeous metallic blue car. I worked second shift at a nursing home as a nurse aide. This was during another time of separation that lasted for months. I exclaimed that I loved that car! Dad asked me if I wanted to go and see it up close, and I said a resounding "YES." We pulled onto the car lot, and there sat the beauty. She was exactly what I was looking for. A shiny Chevy Chevelle Super Sport with leather seats, shiny wheels, and a gorgeous paint job! A car salesman came out and asked us if we wanted to take the car for a test run. Yes, we did. It purred like a kitten. My dad inspected that car from top to bottom, front to back, side to side, inside and out. After getting his stamp of approval, we did the necessary paperwork, and that shiny gorgeous car found a new home. I could hardly believe it! I had graduated from a worn-out, rattly, smelly, old, faded Impala to a sleek, shiny, nearly new Chevelle Super Sport with a 454 engine and dual exhaust! I was ecstatic.

After several months of being apart, my husband called me and told me he missed me and asked me to come back home to him. My parents were not in agreement, but as his wife, I knew that my place was with him.

I moved back with him and got a job at a shoe factory.

My boss was an outrageously mean man. He had a hot temper, had his favorite girls, and I definitely was not one of them. One day, he called me into his office and told me to speed up or he was going to ship me out! I knew that I could not lose this job because I had a shiny new car to pay for, and I was not going to lose that car! I returned to my work station, shaking, scared, hurt, and angry. This action continued for the entire time that I was employed at that factory. No matter how much I produced, it was never good enough. He always wanted more! He told me one day that if I wore more revealing blouses, things might go better for me. I detested him!

Things were rough at home, and I had nobody to talk to about how I was being treated at work. So I talked to God a LOT.

One afternoon, I returned home, and my husband and his mom were waiting for me, along with another girl who was my husband's first cousin. They seemed anxious to speak with me. I wondered what was up. I got out of the car, and my husband told me to get back into my car and follow him. I asked what was going on, and he informed me that we were going to a notary public to sign over my car to his cousin, who had agreed to have my car put in her name and take over the payments. I said that was not going to happen! I loved my car. For the first time in a very long time, I had something that brought me joy, even if it was just a car. But he insisted, pressing me hard to comply, telling me that we could not afford the gas because it had a big engine, and promising me that we would get another car that was more economical and afford-able. His mom stood there like a stone statue, making certain that things went as planned. I learned later that she had a problem with my car because it was newer and nicer than my husband's car. She convinced him that I would use that car to lure men and have affairs. She called it a "stud mobile."

The battle raged in my mind as he insisted that this is how things were going to be. I was in a really tough place. The three of them against me. I was outnumbered, overpowered, and felt that I had no recourse but to comply. You might be asking why I didn't just refuse. Why didn't I get in my beautiful car and go to my parents' house? After so many times of separation, and me showing up at home with all my stuff, and emotions all over the place, my mom had enough! She told my dad that she was not okay with me coming home to stay anymore. I was on my own. He basically told me, "You made your bed. You go and lie in it."

I was hurt, but I knew that I had put them through a lot, and it was time for me to accept the consequences of my awful decisions. Plus, I had vowed to love and cherish this man. Whether or not he chose to uphold his vows, I knew that if I honor my part, God would honor me. That's how I roll!

I lost more than my car that day! I lost so much more. And now I had no way to get to work, or so I thought. I imagined that we would purchase another car for me immediately after signing the papers as my husband had promised, but now that the deal was done, I was left empty and bare. Why was I not surprised? What I did not know was that arrangements had been made with a lady who lived eight miles from us. She agreed for me to come to her house and ride with her to work, but I would have to pay for her gas. I passed her house every day on my way to work, but now I had no car, so how was I to get to her house?

Here's where life gets really, really hard! You talk about the school of hard knocks! I never knew I would ever face a situation like this one. I had no car but was still required to go to work and continue on as usual. When I asked my husband how I was going to get to her house, he told me, "There's nothing wrong with you. You can walk that far."

Eight miles is too far to walk, and it would be pitch-dark in the morning, and it is crossing a mountain! I tried to argue with him, but he wouldn't hear it. He threatened to kick me out of my happy home if I didn't do as he said. I felt more trapped than ever, and now I had no car!

I will never forget the first morning I walked the eight miles to her house. I left our house at four in the morning, armed with only a flashlight. I was young and relatively healthy, and I could speed walk at a pretty good clip. But I was terrified! I have a fear of bears and bulls. Always have as long as I can remember. We lived in-between mountain ranges in dense woods and forest as far as the eye could see. This was bear country. I walked rapidly, making a lot of noise, whistling, singing, hoping to scare off any wild critters that might be in my path.

She was waiting for me to arrive, and when I walked up to her house, she handed the keys for her car to me and asked me to start it so it could warm up a bit. It was a chilly morning. This routine continued for weeks until I got another car. People in the area were aware of my situation and were really talking about it. In fact, they talked about it for years. Just a couple of years back, I was visiting a local county fair. I saw some folks who lived near the lady who gave me a ride to work each day, and as soon as they realized who I was, the older lady in the group told her children and grandchildren that I was the lady who walked over the mountain to go to work. This was forty years after the fact, and people were still talking about it. I remember the feeling I had when she said that about me. It had been so long ago, and, yet, when she mentioned it, it led me down memory lane to that time when I was in a very dark place in my life, a place where I cried out to God for help, for strength, for protection, and for mercy. He gave me all that and more.

Many folks saw me walking, knew my situation, and tried to offer me a ride, but I had been warned that if I got a ride with ANYBODY, it would not end well, especially if it was a man! Eventually, we bought an old Subaru. It was the color of a school bus, but it went well in the snow because of the front-wheel drive. I was grateful to have wheels under me again.

CHAPTER 9

Assuming a New Identity

LIFE WAS VERY DIFFICULT, TO PUT IT mildly. The ongoing abuse and control at home wore away at my mental state. In addition, my boss at work was nearly impossible to please! He regularly called me into his office to tell me that I needed to pick up the pace. I was going as fast as I could, but no matter what I managed to do, it was never enough for him. One day, he called me into his office, yelled at me for not working faster, and told me to get back to work! I stood there for a few seconds, looking for a chance to tell him about my dire circumstances at home, how I had been forced to give up my car, and how I was forced to walk for two hours in the pitch-dark, just to show up at this factory.

My delay enraged him! He shoved two fingers in my chest and screamed, "MOVE, MOVE, MOVE!" He cursed me and shoved me toward the door. That moment, that reprimand, that man sent me into an emotional meltdown. Something rose up inside me and told me to run, run as fast as I can, for as long as I can, as far as I can. Don't think about it, just run! Don't turn around. Don't look back!

At that point, my brain switched to survival mode. I continued to work through the rest of the day, but my mind had traveled to another place far away. In desperation, I hatched a plan of escape.

Over the next few weeks, I researched everything I could find on how to assume a new identity. I would change my name, my hair color, my clothing style, and I would become a new person. I had a plan to drive to a location, abandon my car, board a train under my new alias, and disappear from everything and everyone. A lot of thought went into what my new name would be. I cannot say that I have always loved my name, so this time, I would choose what best fit the new me. I tossed around a few names, saying them over and over to hear how they sounded. I wanted a name that reflected what I was feeling and who I am at the core of my being. I wanted my initials to carry a weight of significance, so I chose the name Sheila Anne Dougherty. The initials are SAD, which is exactly what I wanted the world to see me as—sad.

I mentally said goodbye to my parents, my siblings, my church family, and the few friends that I had. I had managed to save some money on the side, not much, a few dollars here and there, but every little cent was getting me closer to my new identity.

I carried on as usual, went to work every day, attended church regularly, wore a fake smile, and pretended that I was okay. All the while, I was planning my great escape into a new place with a new identity where nobody would know me, where I could finally collect my thoughts, regroup, and start over.

I had reinvented my history in my mind, including my birth date, parents' names, number of siblings, origin of birth, and was prepared to assume a new life. I had plans to work as a waitress, in a faraway place.

How many know that it's a small world and one cannot escape the all-seeing eye of our awesome Creator, God? He saw me furiously planning my escape, and I can imagine He smiled at my persistence, all the while keeping His thumb on my plans. He knew that they would never materialize.

It happened at the altar in the woods. I went there to let God in on my plan to run away and assume a new identity. I even told Him the name I had chosen for myself, so when I came to Him in prayer again, under my alias, He would know who I was. I hadn't given much thought to how He felt about my decision, to be very honest. I didn't think He would object because He saw how much pain I was in, and I needed a break. I finished talking to God and opened my Bible. God immediately got my attention! I had walked into Psalm 139. I began reading slowly, pondering each verse. The Holy Spirit began to speak to my heart. He assured me that He saw me, was intimately aware of the depth of my pain, He watched me as I went to bed and was there all night while I slept. He told me that He greeted me each morning and kissed me awake with His very breath. He said He knew every word I spoke before it formed on my tongue. Then I read verse 7 of chapter 139. The message stopped me in my tracks. God was saying, "I am everywhere. You cannot hide from me. Your running will only delay your healing and your deliverance. I have called you to this place. You are mine. I am with you."

I continued to read the rest of Psalm 139, and I sobbed and wept in God's presence. Reluctantly, I tossed the idea of assuming a new identity. God had shown up that day in the woods. He assured me that He was perfectly pleased with my name, and His plan for my life did not include me identifying as someone else. I knew that if I pursued my plan, God would not bless it. And that was not something that I was willing to risk.

As I look back on that period of my life, I shudder to think about what I would have missed out on if I had insisted on doing things my way. I tremble to think about how I could have fallen victim to predators of every imagination because of my vulnerable state. I cannot even imagine what my life would be like without my family. I am so thankful for the grace of God that redirected me through His Word at that fallen log altar.

I don't know where you are in your walk with God. I have no way of knowing what you have lived through or your current state of affairs, but I do know that God sees you. He has surrounded you on every side. Nothing takes Him by surprise. It is impossible to escape His gaze. So run to Him with your brokenness, cling to Him in your pain, hold on to His promises as if your life depends on it because it does. Pour out your heart to Him. He is waiting to hear from you. Talk to God about everything. He is longing to be welcomed into every moment of your life. Develop an ear to hear His voice. Many voices clamor for our attention, and it is imperative that we are so familiar with the voice of our Good Shepherd that we refuse to follow another.

The voice I heard that day in my boss's office was not God's voice, for the message does not line up with the Word of God. I was so damaged that I could not discern the enemy's voice from God's voice. If I had followed the advice of that voice, I would have been more isolated than ever. Running from my problems was not the will of God for my life. The enemy showed up when I was at my most vulnerable point, and he pushed the right buttons, or should I say, said the right words, and I nearly followed his hideous advice.

God speaks to us in different ways: through His Word, through the Holy Spirit, through prayer, dreams and visions, and people. The important thing to remember is that God's voice is always the same, no matter what avenue He chooses to use. If you are not certain whether or not you are hearing from God, you can fact-check it with His Word. He never contradicts Himself.

"All Scripture is God-breathed and is useful for teaching, rebuking, correcting and training in righteousness, so that the servant of God may be thoroughly equipped for every good work" (2 Timothy 3:16–17).

When we allow the Holy Spirit to rebuke, correct, and train us, we are "transformed into the same image from glory to glory" (2 Corinthians 3:18). We welcome the correction because we know that it trains us for our purpose.

CHAPTER 10

Surprise

IN THE FALL OF 1976, MY DAD called all of us girls into the front room of our farmhouse. We had gathered there for Thanksgiving. He informed us that he had been in failing health for some time now, and his condition was to the point where he could no longer continue the operating of the farm. He asked each of us girls if we wanted to take over the farm. My two older sisters declined right away, and I was torn to my core. That was my home where so many precious memories were made, where the walls rang out with laughter, and so many possibilities could be realized. But I was not in a position to assume such a monumental task of running a dairy farm. My marriage was in deep trouble, and, physically,

I was not in a good place, so I said that I could not take over the farm. My two younger sisters were still in school, so they would not be able to take over the farm.

Public sale was set for March 1977. I had a hard time coming to terms with my parents' decision to sell the farm. I have often wished, since then, that we could have convinced them to live in the house and rent out the land, the cows, the machinery, and keep the farm in our family. But my parents had other plans, so the homestead was sold to a young couple just starting out in life.

Right around this same time, I began feeling ill. I was nauseated all the time and began throwing up a lot. I went to the doctor, certain that I had picked up a virus of some kind. He informed me that I was going to have a baby! Say what? I was ecstatic! I had been praying for a child ever since we got married. You may wonder why I would want to bring a child into this mess? Well, I thought that, perhaps, if we had a child, it would help to snap my husband back to reality, and he would assume responsibility and get a job. I know, it sounds completely foolish now, but then it made sense to me. And, besides, I just knew that I would make a great mom.

I wanted a daughter with all my heart! I envisioned what she would look like all dressed up in frilly lace with ribbons in her hair. I prayed and asked God for a little girl, believing with all my heart that He could do that, but not knowing if He would. But, at any rate, I was going to be a mom! I could not have been more thrilled!

I waited nearly two weeks to tell him that he was going to be a daddy. His response was to scream at me that I had tricked him into this, that he was not in favor of this at all, and that I was entirely on my own! He would have no part in this! With that, he left the house and slammed the door so hard that the pictures flew off the wall. I stood there in utter shock. How did we go from him trying to get me pregnant before marriage, when it was a sin and a transgression before God to this kind of reaction when we are married three years and have God's approval? Nothing made sense. But I was going to be a mommy, and I could not have been happier. It didn't matter what he called me. God had heard my prayer. I didn't care if I had to do this alone. God smiled on me and blessed me with the honor of motherhood.

The pregnancy was rough on many levels. I had hyperemesis, a condition that is similar to morning sickness, but unlike the morning sickness that usually goes away around twelve weeks, hyperemesis does not. It is severe vomiting that leads to weight loss and dehydration. I had to carry a bucket with me everywhere I went. This was right up until I gave birth. My entire pregnancy, I gained only nine pounds, and my baby weighed a little over five pounds, so you can see that it was not a good pregnancy. I am so thankful that she and I both survived.

Once I announced that we were having a baby, the abuse intensified. His mom told him right in front of me that he should sit back and relax and let me work and take care of him. Well, I had been doing that for the past eighteen months. Why tell him that now? I have no idea, except it was meant to cause me stress. It was a reality check for me as I realized he would not be stepping up to the plate and getting a job, not with advice like that.

Within the past year or so, I started getting calls to go to various churches in the area to serve in ministry. I was asked to come and speak for Mother's Day, asked to speak and sing at an Easter service, asked to be the song evangelist at this revival, and come and lead worship for another revival. In spite of all our mess, God was opening doors of opportunity for me to go and minister. Even though we were broken, our marriage was not good, and things were bad at home, God anointed me to sing and speak, and the meetings began to come in little by little.

I was working full-time to support my husband and keep the bills paid and was going out in ministry where God opened the doors. It was a busy life, and God was good.

At my place of employment, where I worked second shift for a while, I received a paycheck every two weeks. My husband and his parents showed up every payday to my employer, collected my paycheck, and I never saw a penny of it. He ran all the finances. I just had to earn the money. He decided if, how, when, and where the money went. He and his mom would shop for our groceries. He never cooked, so I had no idea what he would be bringing home from the grocery store.

As my belly grew, so did his abuse. He would catch me throwing up and say something like, "Looks good on you. This is what you asked for."

His mom had a little song she would bellow out if she saw me having a hard time with nausea and vomiting. It went like this: "If I had listened to what my mama said, I'd be sleeping in a feather bed. Would you do it all over again? Hey, would you do it all over again?"

Seriously, how childish can one be? Oh, and they would all laugh hysterically as I puked my guts up. I got absolutely no support from any of them.

One day, shortly before I gave birth, we had a snowstorm which dumped over a foot of snow, and our driveway was long. I asked my husband to help me shovel snow. He didn't move. I grabbed a shovel and went outside and began to shovel snow. It was wet and heavy. With each shovelful, I felt like I could not continue. I prayed for strength to get the snow removed. It took me over two hours of heavy shoveling to get only one half of the driveway cleared, but it was enough for me to get out onto the road. Not one person came out to help me. They knew I was out there. I saw them peering out every now and then from inside their warm houses, but nobody would come and give me a hand. I remember arriving late to work that day, exhausted, weary, and stressed. I had to travel more than thirty-five miles one way to get to my job, and looming large between my home and my workplace was an unforgiving mountain. It was steep and narrow with no guard rails.

At the bottom, on our side of the mountain, there is a hairpin curve that you have to get around before digging your way to the top. I became very good at navigating that mountain in snow and ice. I carried a set of tire chains in my trunk and used them often to get over that rough terrain. Yes, I lay on my back, on the icy road, after midnight, and put chains on my tires so that I could get home. Life was difficult, but God sustained me. He was teaching me in a dark place. The rocky times of trials became stepping stones as I continued to lean hard on Him and hold on to Him as though my very life depended on it because it did. Oh, it sure did!

I have often heard my father-in-law make the statement that he was thankful that he was not a woman because the women have to do all the work. He used to sit down at the table an hour before mealtime and asked how soon the meal would be ready. He never offered to help with meal prep nor with the cleanup afterward. This is the example that was lived out before my husband and his brother. No wonder he would never lift a finger to help me out, no matter how hard the task or how tired or sick I was. I was his slave.

Our daughter was born in early December 1977. My due date had been December 29, but she decided to come nearly four weeks early. She was tiny, weighing five pounds, three ounces, and measuring eighteen inches in length. She had loads of dark hair, and I named her Angela. She is a gift from God and has been such a blessing to me. I am so thankful for her! God heard my prayer, saw my tears, and gave me what my heart desired.

CHAPTER 11

From Bad to Worse

BEING A NEW MOM WAS SUCH A thrill! I spent hours and hours holding her, just wanting to have her near me. I knew that in a few short weeks, I would be returning to work and was going to make the most of every moment with her.

My husband and his family had stepped up their insults right around the time I announced my pregnancy. It would be twenty-three years before I would get an answer as to why. The answer will shock you. More on that later.

After enjoying six weeks of maternity leave, I very reluctantly returned to work. Ministry opportunities continued to come in slowly. One day, I asked my husband if he would come along with me to watch the baby for me while I sang. He informed me that God had not called him into the ministry. God had called me. He would not be going with me, no matter what the reason. I knew that I was on my own. Somehow, God would give me the wisdom and guidance that I needed. When I went to a church to sing, I would ask the pastor if they had any recommendations of someone in the congregation who could watch my baby girl while I ministered. God always provided just the right lady for the job. My daughter was dragged around from the time she was tiny, from church to church, and she rarely got sick. I think all that travel made her strong. I would get calls to return to churches, year after year, and people loved watching my daughter grow.

I was working full-time, caring for a child, caring for a mentally ill husband, maintaining our home and property, and keeping up with the demands of the ministry. I was burning the candle at both ends. It began to take its toll. My daughter was about two years old when the first symptoms appeared.

The symptoms began as body aches and fatigue. I thought to myself, *Well, it's no wonder. You are pushing your body to the limit. Maybe you need to take a break from some things.* The more I tried to press through, the more my body ached, and the fatigue was overwhelming. I would come home from work so tired that I could not even function. I would have to go straight to bed where I would sleep all night. This continued for months and months. Then I noticed red raised areas around every knuckle on every finger. These areas were very tender, and when I lightly pressed on them, they turned white for a few seconds. Weakness had ravaged my body to the point where I could barely drive to work. I didn't know what was going on.

I worked second shift for over six years and had split break days, meaning that I never had two days off in a row and had to work every weekend. I was missing out on so much of my daughter's childhood and knew that I needed to work different hours if I were to have quality time with her. Second shift worked well for ministry because most of the meetings were Sunday mornings, which I could do because I traveled locally. So I would go and minister in the morning, come home and make lunch, and get ready to go to work. I did that the entire time I worked that shift, and it was taking a toll. I was now dealing with ongoing illness in my body, and the symptoms were becoming increasingly worse.

My husband had no sympathy at all but told me that if I lost my job, I would lose my happy home. So I kept going by the grace of God. One evening, at work, I noticed a job posting for a day shift position. I applied for it and won the bid. I was excited. Life would be so much easier with me working more normal hours.

One morning at work, I was so weak I could not stand up. I slumped to the floor and began to sob. My supervisor ran to me and asked me what was wrong. I told her I was sick. I was taken to the hospital. Tests were run, and I was admitted. My blood work was way out of normal range. My liver enzymes were elevated fifty times the normal level. In fact, the doctor called my parents and told them that if they wanted to see me alive, they should come now because I was in liver failure and would possibly not survive the night.

Prodding and probing, biopsies, scans, and tests all came back inconclusive, but I was dying. My liver was so sick that it was poisoning my body, causing my other organs to fail. Without a miracle from God, I would not survive. I had felt sick for months, but it felt like years to me, so when I got the news that my body was failing, I was not surprised.

They all showed up to see me. I was in isolation, so everyone had to wear a gown and gloves.

My daughter was three years old. She came into my room, bouncing, happy, and bubbly. It was so good to see her doing so well. My parents were standing at the bottom of the bed, and my four sisters were also in my room, scattered about, speaking in low, whispered tones. My husband and his family were in the room as well. I felt my strength fading fast, and I knew I had to have a conversation with my little girl. I asked for her to be lifted up on my bed. I looked in her eyes and told her how much I loved her. I told her that I was going to live with Jesus and she had to be a big girl. I asked her if she could do me a favor and take care of her daddy for me. She nodded her head yes, and said, "Uh-huh."

I gave her a hug and kissed her, telling her how much I loved her. She said, "Love you too." With that, she jumped off the bed and went about mingling with family in the room. I then told my family how much I loved them, but my words came between gasps, slowly, and barely above a whisper. I thanked them for always having my back. I asked them to keep an eye on my little girl for me. Then I could no longer speak. I could see them in the room. I could hear everything that was being said, but I could not speak one word. I prayed in my mind. I told God that I was prepared to live on if that was His plan for my life. I reminded Him that I was only twenty-three years old, and that I felt like I could live a good long time yet, if that was His plan. I also told God that if He was done with me here on earth, if I had accomplished His purpose here, then I was ready to come home to heaven and live with Him.

I will tell you this, as I lay, dying, God flooded my whole being with peace. I cannot explain it, but I felt it. It was total absence of conflict, fear, struggle, or anxiety. Just perfect peace! I have often thought about that peace since then, how it completely enveloped me like wrapping me in a warm blanket. I know that God will not provide dying grace until we are dying. Up until that point, He gives us grace to live.

Then the lights went out. It was very dark. I could still hear everyone in the room, but I could not see a thing. Years earlier, I had been with a group that toured Woodward Cave. It is a walking tour that takes you on a journey deep inside the earth. At one point, the guide turns off the lights. It is pitch-black, absence of ANY light, total and utter darkness. That is what it was like for me as I was entering the coma. But I could still hear. I heard my one sister say to my mom, "If she does not survive this, I will never trust God again."

Inside my head, I was screaming, *Don't say that! You will always need God. He is the only one you should trust. Others will fail you, let you down, betray, and hurt you, but God is ALWAYS faithful, trustworthy, gracious, and merciful.* Then all was quiet.

Suddenly, I heard a sound like two metal objects hitting together. I tried with every ounce of understanding to figure out what it was. Is this heaven? My last cognitive thought was me telling God that I was ready to go to heaven, but I didn't know of anywhere in the Bible that talked about heaven sounding like two metal objects clanging together. I became aware of beeping sounds and whooshing noises and tried to make some sense of it all. Then the lights came on, and it was bright light. The sun was shining in through a window off to my side, and it was bright. My eyes focused, and I noticed that all my family was gone. She was standing at the side of my bed, watching me when the lights came on. She bent down close to my face and shone a small flashlight beam directly into my eyes. She drew in a gasp of air and said in a very excited voice, "You're back!" She ran from the room and returned in seconds with another nurse and a doctor.

Upon examination, the doctor confirmed that I, indeed, had emerged from the coma, and there was much celebration, even with tears, over the fact that I had not passed away. I was in the coma for three days, but God brought me back.

The source of the metal sound that I heard? It was lunchtime, and the nurses were handing out the meal trays. They had metal lids on the trays, and the carts were metal, and they were hitting together as the covers were being removed and placed on a lower shelf on the metal rack. As for the beeping, that was my IV pump, and the whooshing sound was my own heart rhythm on the monitor.

The ability to speak was the last thing to come back. My voice was soft and a bit raspy. I whispered. But I was so weak that I mostly nodded my head. Speaking took so much energy and simply exhausted me. I spoke a lot with my eyes.

Recovery was slow. Diagnosing me with systemic lupus erythematosus would take two more years. I never returned to work. I was simply too sick and weak. On heavy doses of IV prednisone, my body shape and size changed overnight. My weight went from 130 to 210. I was gigantic. My skin was ballooned and stretched, my face was puffy like a chipmunk, my legs and arms were swollen, and when I saw my own reflection, I was unrecognizable.

After thirteen days in the hospital, I was discharged to home. The steroids that had saved my life caused me to gain eighty pounds, and I had to go home in a hospital gown. When I got home, the only piece of clothing that I could wear was a big, floppy, loose-fitting bathrobe. I was devastated. I had never been heavy in my life! I couldn't do this!

God had a plan, He was watching everything unfold, and He was not surprised by any of it. It would take me a while to catch on, but, eventually, I surrendered my pride, my will, and my frustration to Him, and a new beauty began to emerge. It was not a physical beauty; it was an inner beauty that is developed in the darkroom of heartache, pain, and grief. It is a beauty that comes from total surrender to God's will, His way, His timing.

CHAPTER 12

Desperation

WHEN I WAS IN THE HOSPITAL NEAR death, my husband was almost kind to me. I thought that perhaps once I was back on my feet, and he realized how closely he came to losing me that he would have a new appreciation for me. That did not happen. Things grew worse in our home. There was almost constant fighting. We rarely had a decent conversation, even though I longed for that to take place. His first priority was to his parents, and since we lived in their backyard, they were always available to him.

I have never been able to figure out why his mom hated me so much, but I know for a fact that she did. She wanted to be rid of me for years and let it be known in no uncertain terms. She would often say, "No adulterer will make it to heaven, but a murderer can get to heaven." Then she would say, "So you know what you must do."

My mom told me, just a few years ago, that God would wake her often at night and burden her to pray for me. She said God specifically led her to pray for my safety. I don't know how often my life was in danger, but I do know that the enemy wanted to take me out! The enemy hates me, he hates the anointing that I walk in, He hates the destiny that God has for me, he hates my God-given gifts.

At one point in my life, I had sunk into a deep depression that I could not shake. I sought the Lord, cried out to Him day and night, went to my altar in the woods, and poured my heart out to Him with agonizing groans and cries. Yet the depression grew worse. I now realize that what I think was feeding that depression was the intense rejection and abuse from my husband and his family. I decided that I could not continue on any longer. I set a plan in motion that would bring an end to the abuse for good. Over a period of several weeks, I accumulated bottles of sleep aid medication. It was stuff that one can buy over the counter without a prescription. Once I had what I thought to be sufficient to bring my life to an end, I sat at my kitchen table in my tiny house and wrote my parents a letter telling them that I was sorry for all the trouble I had caused them, all the shame I had brought upon our family, and the many ways I had broken their hearts and their trust. I asked them to please know how much I loved them, and that I was sorry for taking this way out of life, but I just couldn't do it anymore. I hurried to the mailbox to get it sent off that day.

That night, as I put my precious little girl in her bed, prayed over her, and kissed her good night, I was convinced that she would be better off without me. Can I just say, right here, that Satan is a liar! My little girl needed me! Oh, how she needed me. And God needed me to be alive so I could continue to fulfill His plan in my life. But in that moment of utter hopelessness, I saw no way out. Once she was safely tucked in, and I had said my goodbyes to her, I went into the kitchen and retrieved the pills from a small box in the cupboard. I sat down at the table and poured the pills out. They were various shapes, sizes, and colors, and I had this crazy idea that this was a colorful way to die.

Then something totally unexpected happened! Somebody was knocking on my front door. Who would be knocking on my door after ten at night? I knew it wasn't my husband because he would not be coming over till later in the morning, if at all. I thought about just ignoring it, hoping whoever it was would just go away, but this person was persistent, and they knocked again. I swept the pills into the small box and placed it back inside the cupboard and went to see who was at my door.

I opened it and, to my surprise, it was my seven-year-old nephew who lived behind us on the property. I asked him what he was doing, and he said he came by to tell me something and to ask me something. I said, "Okay."

He stepped inside the door and said, "I want to tell you how much I love you, and I want to ask you if we can bake cookies tomorrow. My mom doesn't bake, and I am hungry for cookies. I know you make good cookies."

His words pierced the darkness that had engulfed me. The first thought to come to my mind was this, *If I have no other reason to live, I have to live for this little boy.* My eyes filled with tears. I hugged him and called him by name. I told him that we could bake cookies tomorrow. He hugged me back, then turned and ran out the door, calling back over his shoulder, "See you tomorrow."

I was a wreck. I was sobbing so hard I could barely stand. One more time God showed up and saved my life! I went to the cupboard, took out that small box, along with all the pills, walked over to the burn barrel and burned them. As the fire consumed the very thing that would have taken me into eternity that night, all I could do was cry and thank God for saving me one more time!

Two days later, my parents showed up at my house, panic-stricken. They had received the letter I sent them, informing them that by the time they got this letter, I would be in the arms of Jesus. They came tearing into the driveway and burst into the house. I turned to face them, and their eyes were full of questions. We embraced and held each other and cried. I told them the whole story about the pills, about my late-night visitor, and about how God had pulled me from the jaws of death and had given me renewed hope.

My husband was over at his parents' house and saw my dad and mom come flying up the driveway. He and his mom came over to see what all the commotion was about. My mom pulled the letter from her purse and asked my husband if he knew anything about this. He played dumb, but my mother-in-law said that she knew I was suicidal and knew that I was going to kill myself! Even though she knew that, she never reached out to me in any way to pray with me, to show compassion or empathy, just emptiness on her part. My parents never got over that fact, and I struggled with that myself. She was traveling the globe, endeavoring to win the world for Christ, and yet showed no concern whatsoever for me when she was fully aware of my desperate situation.

I know depression is real. And I know that the enemy attacks God's people in many ways. I never would have dreamed that my mind could get to the place where I could not find one reason to go on living. But that is exactly what happened. The Bible says in 1 Corinthians 10:12 (KJV), "Wherefore let him that thinketh he standeth take heed lest he fall." You may be thinking that you are too spiritual to ever succumb to thinking like I did. I say, "Take heed. Beware, for the devil as a roaring lion walketh about seeking whom he may devour" (1 Peter 5:8).

I thank my God of all mercy and grace that He protected me that night. He sent that little boy to my door, when, normally, he would have been in bed, perhaps fast asleep, but here he was at my door, asking me if we could bake cookies the next day! I am still amazed when I think about the saving grace of our loving God. How much He cares for us! His heart is touched by the feeling of our infirmities (Hebrews 4:15), and He rejoices over us with singing (Zephaniah 3:17).

That late-night visit gave me a reprieve from the intense depression. I was still sad, still in a dark place, but the desire to end my life was totally eliminated from my mind. God gave me a desire to live!

CHAPTER 13

The Chicken Is in the Oven

WE CONTINUED TO LIMP ALONG IN A broken marriage, surrounded by dysfunction, coping with mental illness, and holding on to God with all my strength.

My husband experienced many setbacks and needed to be hospitalized to stabilize his mental state, adjust medications, and provide a safe place where he could not hurt himself or anybody else. It was during one of those times that this next event occurred.

I had not been able to work due to my own health issues. Lupus was taking a toll on my body. The struggle was real. My joint pain was such that, at times, I could not hold a toothbrush or comb my hair. The fatigue was excruciating and entire, engulfing my whole body. I needed assistance to get dressed, and doing household chores was nearly impossible. It had been months since my last paycheck, and with no money coming in on a regular basis, things ground to a halt rather quickly. I literally prayed in every cent during those months. It was a course in the school of hard knocks called "living by faith."

Every day, I prayed and sought the Lord to supply our daily bread, and He did. I want to say that it was not in the way I expected or planned, but He always met our needs. I had bills, just like any other household. We had a small mortgage on our trailer and two car payments in addition to the monthly expenses of utilities, groceries, gas, etc. In all those months, I never missed a payment, was never late with any bill, and God always provided. Most times, His provision came in at the last moment, which served to increase my faith.

It was a typical day for my daughter and me. Breakfast that morning was sparse as I recall. Our food supply was pretty much depleted. There was a box of cereal in the cupboard with a handful remaining. I divided it into two bowls and poured the last of the milk over the cereal. As I tossed the empty milk jug into the waste can, I reminded God that I really needed to go for groceries soon.

Later that morning, my little girl was outside, playing in the backyard. It was 10 a.m. She came in and told me she was hungry. There is nothing that moves the heart of a mother like having her children tell her that they are hungry, knowing full well that there is hardly anything in the house to feed them. I asked her what she was hungry for, and she said, "I would love some chicken, please."

I knew there was no chicken in the house, but just to be sure, I opened up the freezer part of the fridge and peered in. Just two ice cube trays, nothing else. Inside the fridge, I saw a small bottle of ketchup with a very tiny amount remaining, a bit of margarine hanging onto the side of a dish, some mayonnaise in a jar, a pitcher of water, and one egg.

I turned to my little girl and told her that we didn't have any chicken in the house and we were going to pray and ask Jesus to provide us with some chicken. We both knelt down in front of the sofa and prayed a short and simple prayer for God to provide the chicken that she was hungry for. We ended our prayer by thanking Him for providing in the name of Jesus.

Now I knew that one egg would not take the place of the chicken, no matter how much I tried, but I took it, broke it into a small pan, and fried it for her to satisfy her hunger for the moment.

She returned to play outside. The Holy Spirit of God impressed upon me to set the table as an act of faith that He was going to supply what we had asked Him for. I obeyed. I set the table with the best dishes we had in the house. But I put out four place settings, instead of two. I could not understand why I felt so strongly about putting out four when there was very obviously just the two of us. I was not expecting company and had not invited anyone for a meal. Just the same, I set the table as instructed by God, and the waiting game began.

Our mail went in the afternoon, with varying times. I had no money, so my heart was praying for God to send some money in the mail that day so I could go to the grocery store, purchase some chicken, and make it for us.

All day long, my heart was in an attitude of prayer, and I was on the lookout for the mailman, certain that he was going to bring me some money. I turned on some worship music and sang along with worship in my heart. As the afternoon wore on, my faith was put to the test. I would look at the table set with four place settings, and my faith would gain strength as I thanked God aloud for His provision. I was eager for the mail to arrive, believing that God was going to answer our short prayer that we had prayed in front of our sofa that morning.

Finally, I heard the familiar mail vehicle approaching, and I ran down the driveway to see what had arrived. I reached into the mailbox and pulled out a light bill, nothing else. At that moment, the enemy attacked with a vengeance. I stared at the bill, knowing that there was no money to pay it, and feeling the emptiness in my own stomach, realizing that I had no way to satisfy my hunger or meet the desire of my daughter for chicken, I walked toward the house slowly, and the attacks came in the form of accusations. "Who do you think you are that God would provide what you need? You are a complete and utter failure as a mother! What are you going to tell your child when she looks at you with hunger in her eyes? God does not care about you! He is willing to stand by and do nothing while you let your daughter starve! You asked for money in the mail, and you got a bill! God does not hear you or see you. Give up!"

I recognized that voice, and I was not going to tolerate him and his evil lies. I rebuked him strongly in the name of Jesus, and told him that he was a liar! I told the enemy that day that God IS my Provider, He SEES me, He KNOWS me, and He WILL ALWAYS be all that I need.

I busied myself with doing little things around the house, frequently looking at the table ready to receive guests, and my faith would be lifted. I filled the atmosphere in our little home with singing, and the hours ticked by. My daughter reminded me that she was still hungry for chicken. I took her by her little shoulders, looked her straight in the eye, and said, "We prayed and asked God for chicken, and we are trusting Him to give us chicken." It satisfied her little heart.

As daylight faded, the enemy tried his best to scatter his lies in my mind and destroy my faith. As the rumbles in my tummy grew, I wondered how God was going to provide, but I leaned hard on Psalm 37:25 where the psalmist says, "I have been young, and now am old; yet have I not seen the righteous forsaken, nor his seed begging bread." That verse gave me the seed of faith that was required to trust God's provision.

Around five that evening, I noticed a car pulling into our driveway. I recognized it as dear friends of mine who lived a couple of miles up the road from us. Their names were George and Jeanette. When

I opened the door, there stood Jeanette, holding a basket that was covered with a linen towel. Behind her, George, her husband, held a roaster in his hands. I was speechless. Jeanette began to speak. She said, "Marilyn, I prepared this meal for George and I, but the Lord asked me to bring it here and share with you and your daughter." Tears flowed as she spoke. My heart was overwhelmed with gratefulness. They came in, Jeanette set the basket on the table, George set the roaster on top of the stove, and while she hugged and kissed my daughter and me, her husband went to the car and brought in a box.

Jeanette looked at the table set for four and asked me how I knew. I told her that I didn't know but felt led by the Holy Spirit, and I simply had walked in obedience.

Our prayers were answered! In the roaster was a roast chicken, golden brown and delicious. The basket was uncovered to reveal Jeanette's own homemade rolls, fresh from the oven. The box held several covered dishes, which contained mashed potatoes, corn, stuffing, and gravy. There was even butter for the rolls and blueberry pie for dessert! God had thought of everything! Oh, how we rejoiced! My daughter did her little happy dance, and I could not get done thanking God for providing one more time. One more time Satan was defeated! One more time God gets all the glory! Hallelujah to God!

We sat around the table that evening in our tiny kitchen and shared that meal with great delight. Our discussion revolved around how this blessing came to be. It is very interesting! Jeanette said, "I took a beef roast out of the freezer and put it in the sink to thaw for supper. But shortly after, I felt impressed to take out a chicken instead. I put the roast back in the freezer and pulled out this big chicken. I thought it would be too much for the two of us to eat at one setting and intended to have leftovers." I asked her if she knew what time it was when she changed her choice of meat for the meal, and she told me it was 10:00 a.m. That is precisely the time that my daughter and I were kneeling at our sofa, praying for chicken.

Just as she pulled the roasted chicken from the oven, God whispered to her to take this meal, box it up, and come and share it with us.

I don't know what you are going through in life. I don't know what you have need of. It may seem as if God does not see you or hear you. Maybe you have prayed for quite a while without getting an answer. Keep on trusting, keep on believing, hold on to your faith in God! When it seems like nothing is happening, *the chicken is in the oven!*

CHAPTER 14

No More

CHRISTMAS ARRIVED. HOW I DREADED THE THOUGHT! I rejoice over the birth of our Lord Jesus, yes, and I am so grateful for the gift of God to the world. But, when times are hard and money is tight, when the family is suffering with illness, when there is abuse, neglect, abandonment, and rejection, emotions run high, and it is not a very joyous season. There was no extra money for gifts that year. I spent a lot of time at my altar during the weeks leading up to Christmas, praying that God would provide for me to buy some Christmas presents. During one of those precious altar moments, God spoke to me and said, "Look around you." I looked at the trees bare of their leaves, I saw evergreens standing straight and tall, dressed in their best, then I looked at the forest floor. I saw a field of trailing pine and instantly knew that God had just answered my prayers.

It was fun gathering that trailing pine, and with each handful, my heart began to fill with hope and joy. I ran throughout the woods, gathering berry sprigs, various types of evergreens, pine cones of all shapes and sizes, and birch twigs. My daughter and I made wreaths, arrangements, and ornaments. Every name on my list would get a gift after all. Thank You, Jesus.

Christmas day was always spent at my in-laws' home. I hadn't spent Christmas with my side of the family for many years. That's just the way it was. My daughter had just turned seven and was in first grade. She was anxious for the Christmas meal to be over and the gifts to be opened.

In the midst of the celebration, there was a cloud of heaviness and apprehension that hung over me. I had been through so much in the past with this family, and I felt like I was always tiptoeing on shards of glass. I was hoping that everyone would receive the gifts that I had invested much time and effort into creating. There was a huge pile of gifts in the corner of their living room, each wrapped in brightly colored Christmas wrap. My daughter, along with her three cousins, sat cross-legged on the floor, each waiting to see what they would receive. Gifts were given out one at a time and always distributed by my husband's mom. One gift would be handed out, and another gift would not be given until the previous one was opened, displayed, and proper thanks was given and acknowledged. It was a long affair, but it was very orderly. I was given several small gifts, but I can't recall what they were. My daughter had been given several small things as well. Her cousins were getting bigger gifts, and she noticed but didn't react.

Then I was given a gift wrapped in a haphazard kind of way. It was covered in different pieces of gift wrap that was taped one on top of the other, overlapping to form a sort of collage. It was not neat at all, but the gift was completely concealed. My mother-in-law threw it at me from across the room and said, "Here, I hope this fits your big back porch." Chuckles and smart comments were thrown around as I opened it to find a dress that was four sizes too large for me, was stretched out of shape, and it was hideous! It was a mixture of paisley prints that looked a lot like the collage of paper that it had been wrapped in. I held it up, and the room erupted in laughter and sneering. My mother-in-law, barely able to speak because she was laughing so hard, told me to go the bathroom and try it on and be sure to come out and model it for them. I felt the tears welling up inside but refused to allow them to burst forth. Someone in the room asked her where she got that dress, and she replied, "From the thrift store."

Now I have no issue with shopping at a thrift store. I love to find a good bargain. But when everyone else was opening expensive dresses from an exquisite store with the price tags still attached, and I was given something that was intended to make me feel cheap, rejected, and less than, I was not impressed. I folded the dress up and laid it on my lap.

The next gift was wrapped in brown paper bags in the same haphazard fashion. This one was given to my daughter. She unwrapped it. Nothing could prepare me for what was in that package! It was a dirty, naked doll. It had rooted hair, which someone had cut down to the scalp, leaving behind rows of stitching and spikes of hair. One eye closed, the other open. Horrified, I tried to keep my emotions in check.

My child got up and brought that dirty, naked doll to me and said, "Mommy, can we give this baby a bath and make her some clothes?" I assured her that is exactly what we could do.

My mother-in-law huffed and puffed and said in disgust, "Well, that didn't work! I was hoping she would throw a fit so I would have a reason to not give the big gift to her. I was hoping to give this to her cousin."

One of the children said, "That doll looks like it belongs in the dump." That is when we learned that is exactly where the doll came from, the local dump!

The rest of that afternoon was pretty much a blur. I was done! I had suffered enough at the hands of these people for nearly twelve years. I made up my mind that I would be making some permanent changes before the new year rolled around. It was one thing to abuse me, call me names, lash out at me, make me the brunt of sick jokes, but when the hostility turned to my child, that was never going to be okay. This mama would do anything to protect her little one. You just had your last laugh at our expense! You will hurt us NO MORE!

Sometimes, God has to kick us in the backside to get us to move. Sometimes, He just plucks us up and places us in a completely different environment.

He knows what He needs to do to get us uncomfortable enough to move. He knew that I could not be free to minister under the stress I was living in. God, in His divine provision, would be our portion as He led us on a path that I never thought would be possible.

I found an apartment, and I, along with my daughter, moved out on December 28 and never looked back. I assured my husband that I loved him, but I would no longer stand back and allow the abuse to continue. He said he understood, but he would not be moving with us. I told him we would keep in touch.

CHAPTER 15

Starting Over

IT WAS NOT EASY LIVING IN THE apartment. We had oil heat, and the apartment was not insulated well. The furnace ran a lot, and we were not very warm. In addition to my rent, I was responsible for the utilities. It proved to be too much. My youngest sister learned of our plight and invited us to come and live with her until we could get on our feet.

February 1985, my daughter and I moved to her home. Things were not ideal. The house was small, but there was laughter, acceptance, protection, and peace. Exactly what we needed. Even though we slept on the floor in the living room, we both woke each morning, fully rested, ready to take on the day. The environment was what made the difference.

We immediately began attending church where my family attended. I loved it, and my daughter was thrilled to be a part of a kids' group. Previously, we had attended small country churches, but this one was large. They offered many options for all ages, areas to get involved in, places to plug into. We were thrilled. Life was good!

I registered my daughter in the new school, and we began a new life in a new place.

We lived with my sister, her husband, and their two children for several months, and then God provided a place for us to call our own.

I joined the church choir, which was amazing, and had occasions to sing a solo now and then. I got involved in a young mother's group called Mom's Time Out. I attended Sunday school and church as well as Wednesday night Bible study. I was flourishing in this new church! God was so good.

My daughter loved her new school, although she was behind in the area of telling time, which she had not yet learned. She picked up quickly and adjusted well, making friends and fitting in. I could not have possibly asked God for anything better.

The call came in from a gentleman in our church, asking me to pray about joining their singing group. It was a family affair. The father played bass guitar and sang tenor, his daughter sang lead and had a beautiful soprano voice, his son played drums, and his wife managed the schedule. They were wanting to add a pianist and a third voice that would produce three-part harmony. They heard me play and sing at church, and God impressed upon them to ask me to become a member of their group.

I joined them, and our harmony was sweet and rich. My daughter and I traveled with them on the weekends for nearly four years. What a precious time we had! The memories we made! The experiences we shared traveling together, singing, laughing, praying, crying! I could write a book on just those four years. How precious those memories are to me today!

God was moving me again. I could feel it, I could sense it. I didn't know where He was moving me to, but I knew He was calling me to some other area of ministry. I began seeking Him with all my heart, asking Him to show me definitely where He was leading. People began to speak into my life that God was calling me to a solo ministry. I fought against it. I was so comfortable, just hopping into the van, settling into a passenger seat, sitting back, relaxed, leaving the driving to the man and his wife, who was our navigator. She read the maps and gave directions. This was way before cell phones or GPS gadgets. We traveled with a US atlas, which contained maps of all fifty states, and included Canada.

I had come from a place of isolation, where friends were forbidden, to a place where I had many friends. I had come from a place of loneliness to a place where I had a strong network of friends around me, friends that were available to me twenty-four hours a day. I had bonded with this family that I traveled with and ministered with. God had blessed us together as a group, allowing us to even go into a studio and make a professional recording. God had given me many songs that I wrote during those years of being on the road with them. I would have been content to continue that path for the rest of my days. But that was not God's plan. I would hold onto His hand, and He would move me on to an area of ministry that would span fourteen years. God was opening another door, and I knew I had to walk through it. I did not know what was on the other side. I just knew that is where He wanted me.

I received a call from my former pastor, the one where I sang in the revival by myself at the age of fifteen. He asked me if I would come and sing for their annual conference. This meant there would be other pastors present, each representing their own congregations. I said, "Yes." I began to pray and ask God for a sign that I knew for sure He was leading me out in a solo ministry and not my own fleshly desire. I asked God to do something that I would know clearly this was His will for me.

The church conference was held for one day. I led worship in the morning and then again in the afternoon. Thirteen pastors, along with select members from each congregation were in attendance. By the end of that day, I had booked meetings with twelve of those pastors! God had shown up again, and with perfect clarity.

I handed in my resignation as pianist and singer the very next day. I was sad to be leaving my friends and that sweet harmony that we enjoyed, but I knew with all certainty that this is what I needed to do. I will never forget the man's response when I handed him my letter. He said, "You just cut my legs off and asked me to run a marathon!" His wife questioned where I thought I would go without them, and I told her I would go everywhere God intended for me to go.

The gifts and calling of God are without repentance (Romans 11:29). Even though I had made poor choices, married outside of His will, and had gotten far off the path He had intended for my feet,

He had moved me into a place where I could once again walk in my calling and shine for my Master. He was asking me to "stir up the gift" (2 Timothy 1:6) that He had put inside of me. The ministry that He had called and equipped me for was about to explode, and I would travel to places I never imagined possible.

CHAPTER 16

Traveling Solo

FOR THE NEXT FOURTEEN YEARS, GOD WOULD take
me on a journey that would zigzag across the US
and into Canada. I had never read a map before and
did not like the idea of traveling alone, but, nevertheless, that is just what I did. The more I traveled,
the more I was forced to read and study maps. The
more I read and studied maps, the easier it became.
God equips those whom He calls.

I began a solo ministry with nothing more than
a notebook full of handwritten songs, a lot of enthu-
siasm, and a whole lot of faith. I came to realize that
God honors humble beginnings.

I had no sound equipment, so I was at the mercy
of what each church had to offer. Can I just tell you

here that I had to minister in some pretty difficult and bizarre situations? One church I remember had a cage around the piano that was made of a metal frame covered in window screen. I was puzzled at the contraption but did not ask any questions. I was told that there was nobody in the congregation to play the piano, so it was played only on rare occasions. The cage was taken off, and the piano was moved away from the wall. I sat down and began to play, and a mouse ran out between the keys, across my hand, and up to the top of the piano where it disappeared over the back. I never even screamed because it happened so fast. I just kept right on singing and never missed a beat. After that service, the piano was pushed back into its position, and there on the floor were several kernels of field corn. The cage that was meant to keep the mice out was lacking a bit in functionality. I think about that every now and then, and it always brings a smile.

One church had a large upright piano that was positioned so that my back was to the congregation the entire time I sang and ministered. That was frustrating, to say the least. I felt like I was singing to a blank wall.

I have played out-of-tune pianos, tiny keyboards, and sung with cheap microphones that made me sound like I was singing into a tin can. In spite of that, God blessed the ministry, and it began to grow.

I prayed a lot about getting my own keyboard and sound equipment. I asked God to provide the money I needed to do that. Little by little, I was able to put money aside. Eventually, God granted my request, and I bought my first sound system and keyboard. What a blessing it has been to have my own equipment.

Traveling for pleasure is one thing, but traveling in ministry is not for the faint of heart. It is not always luxurious. You sleep in many different beds, eat at many different tables, and not everybody cooks the food to your liking, but you eat it anyway and are grateful to have something in your belly. You sleep in homes that have pets, and, sometimes, they jump on you in the middle of the night. You sleep in homes that are so sweltering hot you nearly roast, and, then, you guessed it, you sleep in places where you nearly freeze. You have no control over what is played on the TV or what is blasting from the radio. But you do it all to the glory of God because you realize how blessed you are to be chosen by God to walk in such a glorious calling!

My daughter and I traveled together as much as possible. During the school year, she did not get to go with me as often but did travel with me on the weekends. When summer came, she traveled around with me until fall. Sometimes, she sang with me, which brought me great joy. Most times, she just hung out and helped me carry equipment during the setting up and tearing down process.

Eventually, she would meet the man of her dreams, get married, and start a family of her own. I would continue in ministry, alone again. I cannot tell you how much I missed her.

But God was so good, and He kept on blessing. Doors were continuing to open up, and as I grew in popularity, my datebook became full to overflowing. I was scheduling meetings four and five years out. One year, I ministered away from home fifty out of fifty-two weekends.

My gifts and calling have placed me in front of men and women of influence, and I have ministered to the homeless. I have sung to small groups and have stood before thousands. I have sung in my hometown and have traveled hundreds of miles to minister in one service. I have sung in cathedrals and have spoken from a flatbed wagon, serving as a stage in the middle of a field. I have ministered in air-conditioned concert halls and sung in sweltering tents. I have stood on plush carpeted stages and ministered in a camp meeting where the floor was just ground, which was covered in sawdust. I have sung at onetime events and have ministered in fourteen-day-long camp meetings. I have driven in every sort of weather, and I do not recall any service that I canceled or postponed due to weather conditions.

I know what it is to walk in the anointing of the Holy Spirit. I know the joy of speaking to a crowd and watch them respond as the Holy Spirit ministers to them through the spoken word. I know how it feels to sit at the keyboard and begin to move my fingers under the anointing of the Holy Spirit. I know what it's like to open my mouth and sing under a heavy anointing of the Holy Spirit of God.

All those things are a reality to me. God was blessing, and I looked forward to what He had in store for me. I had no way of knowing that, in just a matter of time, all of this would come to a screeching halt. All that was familiar to me would cease, and the door of ministry would slam shut!

CHAPTER 17

The End of a Chapter

OUR TWENTY-FIFTH ANNIVERSARY WAS APPROACH-ING. IT WAS a huge milestone for us, one that I didn't know if we'd ever realize. Yet, by the grace of God, here we were. I wanted to have some sort of celebration with family and friends who had stood by us as we bumped along, making it to this juncture in our life. Due to the mental illness he suffers from, he was not in favor of doing anything of the kind. He did not do crowds, so we had to keep the number of guests at a minimum. I agreed. I wanted to have a small marriage vow renewal ceremony, hire a photographer to capture the moment, and dress in formal attire. He agreed.

Preparation began for that celebration that was six months away. Our wedding day had been so pathetic and lacked in celebration for a lot of reasons. But here we were, in another season of life. We had managed to stick it out for twenty-five years, which I thought gave us cause to rejoice.

He distanced himself from any of the preparation or planning. I knew he was dragging his feet, but I continued to make phone calls, get prices, and tell those close to me of the plans.

The closer we got to our anniversary, the more apprehensive he became, and, one by one, he began to chip away at the plans I had made. He told me he would not agree to renewing our vows. I wondered why, but he did not have an answer. Then he informed me that there would be no photographer, and he would not be wearing a tuxedo or even a suit. I was disappointed. He asked me how many people were coming to this. When I showed him the invitation list, he told me that I needed to cut that list in half, then he would consider going along with it. I knew he was not going to go through with it, no matter what. I decided to shelf the plans.

The morning of our anniversary came. He got up early and left for the day without telling me where he was going or when to expect him home.

This was his regular routine. He spent nearly every day, running around from here to there, visiting different people, chatting, drinking coffee with them, going to yard sales or anything else his heart desired. He assumed no responsibility around the house, seemed to give little to no thought to our marriage, and lived a carefree life.

I did not see him until the next day. He did not come home at all on our anniversary. I spent the entire evening and night alone. This was a big deal to me. He came home and walked in the house, wearing a sheepish grin. He knew what he had done and seemed to be feeling pretty smug about it.

I asked him where he had been all night, and he replied that he had gone to the home of a friend who invited him to stay for supper. The two of them, both men, chatted away the evening, playing guitar and singing. He said it so matter-of-factly, and that was the way it was. There was no more conversation about our anniversary, the celebration that I had scrapped, or the fact that I spent the night alone.

The next year, our twenty-sixth anniversary came, and he repeated the same exact thing with the same man. By then, I had no expectation that we would do anything special for the occasion. It was just another day in the life. This time, when he returned home, I told him that we were fractured, and we needed to fix what was broken. He told me that there was no way he would go to marriage counseling. He said he wanted out of the marriage. He said he was done with it and just wanted to be free.

In late 1998, I inherited a house from a very dear friend. I chose to move there immediately due to the amount of maintenance and upkeep required for the home, the property, and her many pets. We now had two places to keep up with. My husband came and went as he chose and had complete freedom with no strings attached.

So when he told me on our twenty-sixth anniversary that he was finished with this "marriage thing," I was a bit surprised.

I laid on my face before God and asked Him to heal our marriage. I sought marriage counseling on my own because I needed to be sure that I was being the godly wife God required me to be. I did not want to bring dishonor to the name of Jesus Christ. I was desperate, I fasted and prayed, sought godly counsel from pastors, ran to the Word of God, crying out for God to show up and help me.

One day, I was lying facedown on my living room floor, crying out to God! I needed to know that He had me in the midst of this storm. I told Him that I was not moving until I knew that He had me! I lay there for nearly two days without moving. Desperate people go to desperate measures, and I was desperate! I needed to hear from God! I needed to know that He was with me! My soul was in agony, my heart felt like it was ripped to shreds at the thought of bringing shame and disgrace to God. How could I be a divorced woman and still walk in integrity before men? How could I continue in ministry with the black cloud of a failed marriage hanging over my head? Ministry was my life! God was my world! I felt like such a failure, a complete and utter failure. I had ministered to many others, telling them that God was the answer to their problems, yet could not fix my own. The enemy worked on my mind overtime. I was pleading the blood of Jesus over my thoughts, asking Him to cover me with His righteous right hand.

My Bible was lying beside me on the living room floor, and I opened it up at random, something that I rarely do. I asked God to give me just one tidbit from His Word, just one verse or even one word that would give me strength to stand on for that moment. My Bible opened up to the book of Jeremiah chapter 29. Verse 11 nearly leaped off the page and said, "'For I know what I have planned for you,' says the LORD. 'I have plans to prosper you, not to harm you. I have plans to give you a future filled with hope'" (NET Bible). I breathed a sigh of relief, and as tears of joy swept over my soul and ran down my cheeks, agony was replaced with peace, and the reality that God had me filled me with hope. I got up from the floor, washed up, and got dressed. I had the blessed assurance that I was surrounded by God, like I was all wrapped up in the blanket of His love, and that He was never going to let go of me.

These words from this verse of scripture would prove to be my sustenance for not only that moment, or that day, but for days and weeks to come. To this day, that verse is among my favorites. I cherish the Word of God and hold it dear to my heart.

The divorce was final. And with the end of our marriage, came the end of ministry as I knew it. Word gets around quickly when something like a divorce happens, especially to someone in ministry. Ministers are held to a higher standard, scrutinized with a larger magnifying glass, and put under a more powerful microscope. One by one, meetings were canceled, and I watched as friends walked away, people with whom I had ministered for years distanced themselves from me, and I felt more alone than I had in twenty-six years.

I looked at the datebook I held in my hands and thumbed through the pages that had once been so full of promise, meetings that had been scheduled in good faith now canceled, blackened out, aborted.

I was in the darkroom!

CHAPTER 18

I Get Some Answers

THROUGHOUT OUR MARRIAGE, AND EVEN WHEN WE were still dating, I had the nagging feeling that my husband did not love and, perhaps, had never loved me. I never felt protected by him, and he never once defended me against the many onslaughts of name-calling, jeering, scoffing, and ganging up on me by his family. I felt vulnerable, abandoned, and unloved.

Now that the divorce was final, I wanted some answers, and I would not stop until I had what I had been searching so many years for.

I asked him why he married me. I told him that he could have married any girl he wanted. He looked down at the ground and refused to speak, and I pressed him for an answer. I wanted to know why he would marry me if there was no love there. Finally, he blurted out, "I had to marry you!" I told him that was absolutely ridiculous! He was never under any obligation from my end of things to marry me. Nobody forced him to marry me. How could he say such a thing? I needed to know more, so I questioned why he made that statement. Again, he reiterated the fact that he had to marry me. I asked him who told him that he had to marry me. He said, "My mom."

Out of all his family, it was his mom who treated me the worst. From the morning she slithered up to me at the stove and told me that her son would love her more than he would ever love me, I knew she was not a friend of my marriage.

Now he told me that she was the one who made him marry me! It made no sense, and I told him he had to give me a better answer than that. I reminded him of how she had mistreated me, how I felt like she hated me from day one. Why in the world would she tell him that he had to marry me? He told me that I wouldn't understand.

I assured him that I would try my best to understand and told him that I deserved to know the truth. After all that I suffered through, I at least deserved to know the truth behind the suffering.

He said two words that would throw me for a loop. I never saw it coming. I could not have prepared for what he said next. I asked him again why his mom would make him marry me, and he said, "The farm." The farm? What farm? "Your farm, your dad's farm." I fell silent in shock and disbelief. My mind was reeling, and I was groping for words but found none. The farm! What could our farm possibly have to do with her forcing him to marry me? I finally found my voice and asked him what the connection was between our farm and our marriage? He said that when she found out from my pastor that my parents owned a farm, from that day, she coaxed him to marry me, believing, hoping that someday, somehow, that farm would be hers. Wow, his words left me stunned in a state of mental paralysis. Then, all of a sudden, it all started to make sense.

From the day our farm was sold, the abuse from him and his family intensified, and no matter how I had tried to reason it out, think it through, process it all, it remained beyond my understanding. I know that I am far from perfect and have made lots of mistakes, but I have always made an effort to be kind and courteous, giving the benefit of the doubt, forgiving often and quickly, striving to keep the peace as much as possible.

Once our farm was no longer a playing card in her hand, she changed her strategy. My mind went back to the first time I heard her tell my husband that no adulterer could make it to heaven, but a murderer could. Then she casually dropped the bomb by adding, "You know what you've got to do." Honestly, I was so naive, and, at the time, I thought she was telling him to repent and make sure his heart was right with God. Now I could see that she was throwing a huge hint to get him out of a marriage that no longer fit her narrative. She never wanted me as a daughter-in-law, she wanted my dad's farm. Somehow, she had assumed that I would eventually inherit it from my parents, and since he was married to me, it would be half his, and through her son, she would gain access to our farm.

The conversation continued, and I asked him to be straight up with me about why he wanted the divorce. Usually, people seek a divorce in order to gain some kind of freedom. I reminded him that he had complete freedom in our marriage to do whatever he chose to do—did not hold down a job, always had a nice vehicle, even though he didn't work, lived like a single man with no obligation, and seemed to be relatively content. He was obviously struggling to find the words, and when he spoke, it was just above a whisper. I strained to hear what he said. "I had to." I pressed him to tell me more. I asked him if he was seeing another woman. He assured me that he was not. So the next question, of course, was, "Why did you have to divorce me? I know that it wasn't your mom pressing you to do this, so what is really going on here? What could you possibly hope to gain by getting divorced?"

He told me that the voices inside his head were instructing him. I encouraged him to keep talking. "The voices have been in my head for years. Early on, I could ignore them, shut them up, resist them. But, over time, they became louder, stronger, and I could no longer ignore them," he said. So what exactly were the voices telling him? That is the question. I posed the question and braced myself for the answer. He told me the voices were telling him to get rid of me at any cost because when he got rid of me, he would be healed. He had believed all these years that I was the cause of his mental illness. I was the problem, and the solution was to get rid of me.

He was a torn and conflicted individual. On one side of the conflict, the voices in his head tormented him to get rid of me, while on the other side of the battle, his mom repeated, over and over, that no adulterer could go to heaven, all the while urging him to get rid of me. What was he to do?

Suddenly, the light came on. I understood clearly why he was so intent on bullying, abusing, jeering, belittling, wounding, hurting me. His intentions, way back when our marriage was in its infancy, were to drive me to get divorced from him or commit suicide so he could be healed. When neither of those things materialized, he switched gears, and things became extremely serious. I won't go into detail because this book is not about retribution. It is about bringing glory to God. Let me just say that I am deeply and painfully aware of three different instances where he tried to take my life, and, each time, God intervened, stepped in, and spared my life. God is my Protector, and He saved me from certain death on many occasions. I give Him all praise and thanks!

CHAPTER 19

Growing in the Dark

WITH THE DOORS OF MINISTRY CLOSED, MY voice silenced, my influence diminished, hidden away from view of the public, in a silent and dark room, God had my full attention. I was finally in the place where He would develop me into the person He could trust with the gifts He had deposited in me.

With my focus of DOING FOR God, I began concentrating on BEING WITH God. What a difference! I was learning how to sit at His feet, look into His face, study His character, and immerse myself in the Word. Even though I always had a love for reading the Bible, my desire to study the Word became my passion. The Bible says that Jesus IS the WORD. In the beginning was the Word, and the Word was with

God, and the Word was God. That Word became flesh and dwelt among us, and we beheld His glory, the glory of the only begotten of the Father, full of grace and truth (John 1:1, 14). When we get into the Word and get the Word into us, we are growing our relationship with Jesus. He is the very Word of God. Become a partaker of the Word of God, not just a casual reader. It will change your life.

Little by little, God gently nudged me, never in a condemning way, always in love. His precious Holy Spirit is my Teacher, and so I would learn many life lessons there in the darkroom. Sometimes, the darkness weighed so heavily on my soul that it felt like it was crushing the very life out of me. I could not see my hand in front of my face, and fear and anxiety would creep in to steal my peace. All my life, my identity was in what I did for God in ministry. I realize now, that was a misplaced identity, planted in my thoughts by the enemy of my soul. My true identity has nothing to do with my service. My identity is who I am in Christ and who Christ is in me. Lessons learned in the darkroom would serve to transition me into who God required me to be.

One of many places God took me in the darkroom was to a whole new level in worship. When I mention the word *worship*, what comes to mind?

Often, we think of worship as singing with hands raised in the air. But, sometimes, the greatest posture of worship is a soul who is crushed but chooses to worship God anyhow! Can I tell you my soul was crushed and broken? I felt like I was gasping for my very breath. And yet God stirred me into worship in the midst of the pain. I always loved to sing and play the piano, but now I was learning how to worship. Worship prepares the atmosphere for God to move on our behalf. Worship breaks down walls that separate us from God. Worship is a lifestyle, not an event. Worship is shifting our focus from doing to being. Worship is complete surrender of one's will and life to God and His purpose (Romans 12:1).

Waiting is one of the hardest and most frustrating things for us to do. It is not comfortable, is not gratifying in any way, and has negative connotations attached to it. God has taught me some valuable lessons about waiting. What we do while we wait is of utmost importance. How we wait is a direct result of our level of maturity. If we want to throw a temper tantrum, all the world will see us as the toddler that we are. When waiting causes us to get uptight and tense, then it is obvious that we still have not learned the art and may need to repeat that class until we get it right. Why is waiting important? It is in the waiting that our priorities become clear. My priority prior to the darkroom was to stay busy in ministry. In fact, ministry robbed me of my relationship with God, all because I did not have my priorities straight. So God removed me from ministry for a season so I could get my priorities in their proper order. Waiting properly helps us develop perseverance.

Perseverance is defined as "persistence in doing something despite difficulty or delay in achieving success." Persevering in the waiting room of God develops spiritual muscles so when we complete the course, we are ready for the next season. I was in a course of waiting, and God taught me to persevere in faith while I waited.

God grew me up in patience. I was in a position where I had no way to change my situation. Only God could promote and move me to the next level. I needed to become the best student possible and learn all I could about what it means to be patient. Patience is vital to our survival. Patience is a fruit that the Holy Spirit wants to grow in each of us. In order for the fruit of the Spirit to be displayed in our lives, we need to be connected to the Vine. Jesus tells us that He is the Vine, we are the branches. Before the darkroom experience, I thoroughly believed that I was abiding in the Vine but came to realize that I was putting in a whole lot of effort to produce fruit on my own. God showed me the error of my ways by pointing out that it is not in striving but rather in abiding that fruit is produced. When we are abiding in the Vine, all striving ceases, and we submit to God's perfect timing. Patience is a beautiful fruit of the Spirit. Patience produces character, which produces hope, and that hope does not disappoint because the love of God is poured out in our hearts through the Holy Spirit (Romans 5:1–5).

Humility was a hard pill to swallow. For twenty-six years, I had traveled in ministry to some degree, singing, speaking, leading worship. I was well-known in the community for being a ministry of song and spoken word. It's who I was. People respected my position and held me to a higher standard. When I was silenced and put in an obscure place, I had to face the humility of being demoted. I heard their whispers, was on the receiving end of their judgment, and felt the sting of their alienation. I was humbled. God taught me to not only swallow my pride, but He showed me how to walk in humility before Him and my fellowmen. Humility is often associated with being passive or insecure, but this couldn't be further from the truth. Humble people are confident in who they are and do not resort to boasting. Walking in humility meant that I was going to allow God to promote me without my help. I am so grateful to God for the way He grew me up in humility.

God gave me twenty-twenty vision. When you find yourself in the thick of the battle, it is hard to see what is going on. You are consumed with fighting to stay alive. When you are put in a dark place, you might be tempted like I was to have a backward glance. I spent so many years looking back at my pain that I did not notice the blessing of today. Nobody can drive safely down the road by only looking in the rearview mirror. That is what I was attempting to do, and it nearly wrecked me into the ditch. God spoke to Moses and told him that His name is I AM (Exodus 3:14). He is a very present God. His name isn't I WAS, nor is it I WILL BE. He said I AM.

While I spent so much time looking back, I was missing out on what God was doing in the present. Sometimes, when you are in a dark place, and it looks like you're being buried, it is then that God is planting you. My vision changed in the darkroom as I began to see my situation through the Word of

God and apply TRUTH that lives there. As truth took root in my heart, the light began to shine brighter and brighter, revealing the ugly lies of the enemy that I had come to believe. It did not happen in a moment, but rather, my vision improved in little snippets of revelation over a period of many years.

CHAPTER 20

I Am a Joseph

It took me a while to regroup. I knew I had to find a new source of income, so I began seeking God about what He would have me do. That's when I met up with her. She was a former teacher of mine from public high school. I loved her, and we had a great relationship. I was excited to see her as it had been many years since we last talked. She told me she heard about the divorce and asked me what I was doing, where I was living, where I was working. I told her I was seeking God about where to work. She told me she was looking for a cleaning lady and would love to have me come and clean her house. She also told me that she had three other ladies in her neighborhood that were looking for a cleaning lady but were hesitant to hire one due to trust issues. She assured me that they would all love me, and that I should consider her offer. I promised her that I would pray about it and let her know shortly. Over the next few days, I made it a matter of prayer and felt that God was telling me to go ahead and give cleaning a shot. I called the teacher, told her of my decision, and, soon, I was cleaning five days a week. God blessed that effort, and it became full-time work in a matter of weeks.

Life settled into a routine of work and babysitting my grandchildren. Oh, how I loved helping to raise my grandbabies! In spite of my life being so full, my heart was lonely, and I began longing for companionship of a man. I wanted to have a second chance at marriage if God would allow it. I began to express my heart to God and tell Him what I was feeling. I even gave him a list of physical traits I wanted. I can just imagine Him chuckling over that one because He had my future already planned, and my next husband did not look like I had envisioned. Thank God that He doesn't always give us what we ask for!

I began casually dating men that I met on a Christian website. They were local men who claimed to be Christians. Dating was a nightmare.

I hated that whole process of putting yourself out there, only to have some wise guy come along and cut you deep in your heart. Every man I dated was wounded in some way and bouncing back from a recent divorce. After six months of that nonsense, I was done. I told God I had changed my mind about being married again. I told Him that I obviously didn't have enough intelligence to choose my mate, so I was not going on one more date. If and when I was to meet my husband, God would have to drop him into my lap.

October 31 is when I met him. I had been busy with laundry and was back and forth between the living room and the laundry room, drying clothes, and putting them away. I was online for a bit, then went to the laundry room to check if the last load of laundry was dry. When I returned to the living room, there was a notice that someone was waiting to chat with me. Reluctantly, I clicked on the notice. It was somebody who found my profile on the Christian website, and his message said: "I need to talk to you."

My first thought was, *Oh no, another desperate man, just what I don't need.* But something inside me said, "Give him a chance." We chatted for a while online, then he asked me if he could call me. I said,

"Yes." We talked on the phone for over four hours. As I listened to him talking about his love for God and his children, I fell in love with his heart. At the end of that conversation, he asked me if he could pray for me. My heart was deeply touched, and I was moved to tears. God knew what He was doing.

I lived in the US, and he lived in Canada. I had asked God for white sand and palm trees. He gave me white snow and pine trees. We may think we know what we want, but God knows exactly what we need. I must say, our connection was strong from that first conversation, and every time we spoke, he prayed for me and over me. We fell in love, and I was ecstatic! God was still teaching me so much in the darkroom. But I will never forget one particular night He rocked my world.

We had been dating long-distance for nearly a year. Plans were being made for us to marry. However, it was not decided where we would reside after marriage. During one conversation, he said he would move to the US to live and would seek immigration here. I liked that idea because that meant I did not have to sell my house, get rid of my pets, pack up, and move. During prayer, I was earnestly seeking God as to where He wanted us to live. I asked God to speak to me clearly because this was a really big deal. This is what God dropped into my spirit: "You are a Joseph!" I told you He rocked my world. Okay, first of all, I am a female, and Joseph is clearly male. Second, what does Joseph have to do with where we are to reside after marriage? Silence. Not another word from God. I waited, prayed, asked Him to speak again. Nothing. So I am a Joseph. What could that possibly mean? What was I to do with that tidbit of information? I opened my Bible and began to study the life of Joseph. It made no sense that I would be a Joseph, but that is clearly what I heard.

During our next conversation, I shared with my husband-to-be about the Joseph thing. He told me that some lady from his church told him that God was asking him to remain in Canada for the sake of his two children who were estranged from him at the time. That's when we decided that perhaps my being a Joseph meant that I would somehow be instrumental in resolving the conflict between him and his children.

Plans were made. We would be married, and I would move to Canada.

On September 14, 2002, we were married, and following a short honeymoon, we settled down in Canada. We were both so happy. We attended my husband's church where I became involved with worship, playing piano, and serving on the worship team. It was like a breath of fresh air.

We were deliberate in carving out time for his children—a son who was fifteen and a daughter age thirteen. They did not receive me well and were not open to the idea of spending much time at our house. Over time, his son would make the decision to live with us full-time. But his daughter became more and more distant and eventually refused to see her dad at all.

Two years after we moved to Canada, we both felt that God was moving us back to the US. My dad's health was failing, and taking care of him had become too much for Mom. My grandchildren were growing up without me, and that broke my heart. So the decision was made to move to the US. We put our home on the market, packed up, and moved to the US.

What does this have to do with me being a Joseph? Well, I was confused about that whole thing. My plan of reuniting my husband and his children only worked for the half. His son made the decision to move with us, but his daughter moved nearly six hours away, so the chances of building a relationship with her quickly faded.

Whatever God meant by telling me that I was a Joseph, it wasn't reuniting my husband with his children.

I sought God different times, asking for more information about how I am a Joseph, but all was quiet.

When we moved to the US, we lived with my parents for a while until we found a home to purchase. Then we settled in, and life took on a new normal. In the daily routine of life, I thought less and less about me being a Joseph. Yes, the thought would surface every once in a while, but I did not dwell on it much and rarely asked God for more information. I just kind of stored it in the back of my brain, and life went on.

Dad's health declined, and I became his caregiver. I lived with my parents 24-7, and my sole responsibility was to provide the care my dad needed. As his health deteriorated, we had a visiting hospice nurse who would come to the house twice a week. On the day Dad passed away, she was called to come and pronounce him deceased. She stood at the bottom of his bed and told me what a great job I had done in caring for dad. She remarked how I cared for him so gently, yet thoroughly. Then she told me that the agency she worked for was looking

176

to hire another nurse aid and told me I should consider applying for the position. I thanked her and told her I would give it some thought.

After Dad's funeral, I did apply for that position and was hired immediately. I worked for that agency as a home health and hospice nurse assistant. I loved my job. One day, I was called into the office. They were offering me an opportunity to go to nursing school, and they would help with tuition. I was so excited.

I applied and was accepted into nursing school. Two months after starting school, the agency was bought out by another company who did not honor the agreement to pay tuition, so I was on my own.

I graduated nursing school and, shortly after graduation, sat for my state board exam. I passed on the first attempt and breathed a huge sigh of relief.

I was hired on a med/surg floor, and I loved my job. I worked with an amazing team of nurses who became like family.

One day, I had a patient who was gravely ill. She had quite a few visitors in and out of her room, and I felt the urgency to pray for her. I told God that I would like to go and pray with her, but she had visitors hovering over her. I asked Him to make a way for me to go and pray with her. Within moments, everyone cleared out of her room, walked past the nurse station, and announced that they were going to get something to eat, and would be back in about an hour or so. I whispered, "Thank You, Lord" and hurried back the hall to her room. I stuck my head around the door and greeted her. She smiled as I walked up to the side of her bed. I looked at her and asked her if she would mind if I prayed for her. She was thrilled and grabbed my hand as I began to pray. I don't remember what I prayed. I think it was a simple prayer, probably not a very long prayer. But I will never forget what she said back to me.

She looked at me and said, "Now I have something to tell you. It makes no sense. I have no idea what it means, but God is telling me to tell you something. I can't even believe that He is wanting me to tell you this because it makes no sense, and I have never done anything like this before in my life!"

I looked at her and said, "It's okay, go ahead and tell me what God has laid on your heart."

She said, "Well, this makes no sense to me, but perhaps you will understand what this means. God says to tell you that you are a Joseph!"

I immediately asked her if God had told her anything else, and she said, "No," that's all she got.

Ten years had passed since God dropped that into my spirit. Ten years God had been silent about it, and now my very ill patient told me I was a Joseph!

She asked me if it made sense to me. I was a mess! I couldn't stop the tears. They ran down my face, and she thought she said something wrong. I assured her that she had not. I sought the Lord and asked Him to reveal more about how I am a Joseph, but He would remain silent on the subject for another season.

Two years go by without another hint about how I am a Joseph. One particular day, I got to work, received the shift-change report from the previous nurse, and assumed responsibility for the patients in my care. One of my patients was suffering from liver failure and, without a new liver, would not survive. She was a Christian, and her attitude about her situation was remarkable. She told me that she was not worried about whether she received a new liver or not because, either way, she wins. If she gets a new liver, she gets to live a little longer, but if she did not receive a new liver, she would get to go to heaven sooner than later. "Either way," she told me, "I win."

I wanted to pray for her, but her husband and her sister were with her, and they would be staying all night. I felt God impressing me to minister to her, but I needed the room to be clear for me to do that. I stood at my med cart and prayed that God would allow a few moments for me to pray with her. Within a few moments, both of her visitors walked out of her room, and passed me, stating that they were going to go for supper. I thanked God for answering my prayer and hurried toward her room. As I neared her door, I heard God say to me, "I want you to sing over her." I walked through her door and approached her bed. I told her that I had intended to come in and pray for her, but God had told me to sing instead. I asked her if she minded if I sang over her. She replied, "No, not at all! Please go ahead."

I started to sing, "I am the God that healeth thee, I am the Lord, your healer. I sent my word and healed your disease. I am the Lord, your healer."

Tears welled up in her eyes and spilled on to her cheeks, and I continued. I told her, "Now this is your response back to God. You are the God that healeth me, You are the Lord, my healer. You sent Your word and healed my disease, You are the Lord, my healer."

Can I just tell you, God came in that room in a powerful way! His presence was real, and it was amazing. She told me she had never heard that chorus before, and she loved it. She asked me to sing it again, so I did. She had me write the words down for her so she could share it with her husband and her sister when they returned. Then she got a puzzled look on her face. I asked her if she was all right. She said she was, but she had something to tell me. I said, "Okay, what is it?"

She said, "This makes no sense, and I don't understand it at all."

I had an instant flashback to the patient two years prior who had begun a conversation the same way. I told her to go ahead and say what was on her heart. I was God's child, and she was God's child, and whatever He wanted her to tell me would be okay. She looked at me and said, "God is telling me to tell you that you are a Joseph."

I was a wreck. I plunked right down at the foot of her bed and told her that I was not leaving that room until I had more. I needed to hear more about it. She then proceeded to tell me that just as Joseph was put in prison, in a dark place, lonely and forgotten, God had placed me in a darkroom where He was developing me, and when the time was right,

He would bring me out of that dark place, into the light where He would promote me to the next level.

Twelve years after dropping that into my spirit, I finally get to see more of the picture. I will tell you this: after that dear patient spoke those words to me that day, my focus shifted. Her words confirmed the fact that I was, indeed, put in a darkroom. I was, however, surprised to hear why I was in the darkroom. I was placed there out of God's great love, in order to grow me up, to develop me into a vessel worthy to bear His name, and to shape my character in order to produce the fruit of the Spirit and reflect my heavenly Father. I was still carrying too much junk around in my heart from my past, and it was hindering me from getting to the place where God could trust me to carry the heavy anointing that He would have me walk in.

Eight more years would slip through the hands of time before my situation would begin to change. In that chapter, I would become a better student, eager to learn, ready to grow and evolve, but there was still so much I had to learn.

CHAPTER 21

Holding on with Fervent Faith

I WAS ON A MISSION TO LEARN as much as I could, in the shortest time possible, to show God that He could trust me with the gifts and calling that I was given. But God is never in a hurry. He doesn't punch a time clock, and He was not moved by my eagerness to graduate early. I would be required to stay in class, in the darkroom, until HE decided I had passed the tests and met all His conditions.

I became intentional about my relationship with Jesus Christ. He became my top priority. My prayer life changed dramatically. I now pray deliberately and specifically, rather than in generalities.

I have learned to walk in humility before my God who sees me, knows me intimately, and loves me unconditionally. I am keenly aware of the weight of responsibility that I bear because of the talents, gifts, and calling He has placed on my life. I will be required to give an account to Him for what I do with what has been given to me. "To whom much is given, much more will be required" (Luke 12:48). Lord, help me, Jesus!

The closer I press to God, the more He reveals His love to me. Even as I am writing this book, I am praying for wisdom over each thought, each word, each sentence. The Holy Spirit is my inspiration, my teacher, my guide. He knows what needs to be written on these pages, and He knows what should not be mentioned.

Every once in a while, God allowed me to sing or speak at a church or event during those years in the darkroom. Such is the case here. I was called upon to speak at a women's retreat. I will never forget the joy I got from that call. Perhaps God really had noticed me after all. Maybe He was going to open doors of ministry now, and this was a new beginning. My hope was renewed. I prayed and studied in preparation for the retreat. God clearly spoke to me about what to share with the women.

I remember sitting outside the building where the event was scheduled. It began on a Friday evening and ended the next afternoon. I arrived early and had some extra time. I sat in my car and began to pray. I thanked God for the opportunity to minister to the ladies, to one more time shine for Him. I reminded God that it was only by His grace that I was there in that very spot. I was expecting to give these women a wonderful word from God, delivered under the anointing of the Holy Spirit. God did not disappoint.

It was the first worship service of the retreat, and I was standing at the back of the room, entering into worship. My eyes were closed, and I was focused on worshipping God, and I felt a tap on my shoulder. She was a young lady, probably in her twenties. She was trembling and asked me if she could speak to me. I assured her that she could. The music and worship were loud in that place. She began to speak, but I was not able to understand what she was saying. Suddenly, she reached out and embraced me and spoke right in my ear. She told me she was a brand-new baby Christian, and she had never done this kind of thing before, but she had felt God so strongly impressing her to give me a message. She said when the worship music started, God told her to give me a message, but she resisted. The longer the worship continued, the louder the message was in her heart until she could no longer contain it. She was extremely nervous, trembling from head to toes, and she wrapped her arms around me tightly. It seemed that she was holding tightly to me so she wouldn't fall over.

I encouraged her to deliver the message God had given her for me. She told me she was very nervous, and I told her that God was right here between us, among us, and in us, so it was okay. She began to speak. I don't remember her message word for word, but it was something like this:

> God wants you to know that He sees you. He hears your prayers. You have been in an isolated place for a long time, and God is getting you ready to bring you out on display again. He is restoring your ministry. New doors are opening for you. A new and more powerful anointing is going to be poured out on you. He says your ministry will be seven times greater than it was before. Get ready, get ready, get ready!

I was pumped, super excited to have received that word from God that night! I fully anticipated that calls would come pouring in, the datebook would start filling up with scheduled meetings. I was ready to walk through the open doors before me, to walk in the new anointing promised.

After that retreat, the meetings did not come in, the datebook was empty, my heart was breaking, and my mind was troubled. Had I misunderstood? Is there something wrong with me? What is going on?

I continued to seek God, to surrender all of me to Him—my past, my present, my future, my gifts, talents, calling, my hopes, my dreams—all of me I laid at His feet.

This event took place in 2008. As I write this, that was fifteen years ago.

God in His infinite wisdom knew that I still had a lot of growing up to do before I would be ready for promotion.

It would require me to let go; I had held on to the wheel of control, and I needed to let that go. I was clinging tightly to self-confidence, trusting in my own capabilities, relying on my own strength, and I needed to learn to lean solely on God and not my own understanding.

I would be required to surrender my pride, my will, my agenda, my schedule, my gifts, my calling, and myself to His correction and His instruction. The fact is, I am always learning, and the more I learn, the more I realize I've got so much more to learn.

I would learn that I had to take hold; in order for me to grow in that dark place, it was imperative for me to hold on to the truth of God's Word, and not only hold on to it, but I needed to make it mine. I need to own the Word. It is the living Word of God, my bread of life. Growth happens when we eat. If we stop eating, we starve. The same is true spiritually. The Word of God is a huge banquet table prepared for us individually. We need to pull up to that table and feast on the rich Word of God, to take it in, ingest it, chew on it, meditate on it, commit it to memory. And in the months and years to come, I would need to grab hold of faith. Faith in God, in His timing, in His providence. I would need to hold on with fervent faith.

CHAPTER 22

Random Things I Learned

UP TO THIS POINT, I HAVE ENDEAVORED to record events and happenings of my life in chronological order as much as possible.

For this next chapter, I am going to take the liberty of writing down random things I have learned in the sixty-five years that I have been on this earth. These lessons are in no particular order, but they all carry significance.

Things are rarely as they appear, so don't be too quick in forming an opinion or be tempted to judge.

Bathe every decision in prayer, and don't move until God gives you the green light. He sees what is just beyond the bend, and it is in your best interest to trust His timing in all things.

I have a deeper understanding of how I am a Joseph. I am more like him than I could imagine. Here are some interesting comparisons:

Joseph was seventeen years old when his brothers plotted to kill him along with his dream.

I was seventeen years old when Satan made an attempt to kill my dream and my destiny.

Joseph was betrayed by his own family. I was betrayed by my husband and his family.

When Joseph was thrown into the pit, it looked like his dream had died, but that is not the case. When I faced divorce, it looked like my dream had died, but that dream is very much alive and well.

Joseph's life would take many twists and turns, and my life did as well.

Joseph was imprisoned and forgotten about for many years. I was held in the darkroom for many years, and people forgot about me.

Joseph made several attempts to draw attention to himself while being held in prison on false pretense. I did the same thing. I knew God had placed me in a darkroom, on a shelf, and yet I tried to get noticed. I would casually drop a hint here and there concerning my gifts and calling, hoping that someone would recognize the truth of who I am, but to no avail. As long as I am trying, God is not in control. I need to trust Him, trust in His timing to work ALL things out. He is an on-time God.

Joseph was brought out of prison when God knew that he was ready for the huge task of saving an entire nation. God is going to bring me out of the darkroom when He knows I am ready for the task ahead.

As Joseph faced his brothers all those years later, they feared for their lives. They were afraid he would have them killed for the way they treated him, but he had completely forgiven them. He looked at them and said, "What you meant for evil, God used for good." That is exactly how I feel about how I was treated. The enemy meant to harm me, to stop me, to silence my voice, steal my dream, and kill my destiny, but God used all of the pain for my good! Hallelujah! To God be the glory, to God be the glory, to God be the glory for the things He has done!

Only God knows what task lies ahead for me, but He has been giving me hints along the way. Recently, people have begun to speak into my life more frequently. God is speaking to me through people I don't even know. I love how God works. He is showing me glimpses of what is in store, and it is exciting. He is opening doors that I never dreamed possible. My gifts make room for me. The world will not understand what is happening when God promotes me. I need to keep my eyes focused on God, not looking to the right or the left. God is taking me to a new dimension. I am being told to activate, activate, activate!

Be careful who you share your dream with; not everybody will be able to receive it, understand it, or support you in it. I call them dream snatchers.

People will hate you because of the anointing you carry. They pretend to be your friend but are secretly jealous of the way the Holy Spirit flows from you.

All the forces of darkness cannot stop what God has ordained.

Never judge the book by the chapter you walk into.

Isolation is the first thing the enemy does to defeat us.

Wisdom is a treasure from God. He promises to give it to us liberally. He will not grant wisdom to immature people. I grow in wisdom at the same rate I grow in spiritual maturity.

I had to learn to identify the real enemy. For many years, I was convinced that my ex-husband and his mom were my enemies. I had many reasons to believe that, but I was wrong. We all share a common enemy. He showed up a long time ago in a garden called Eden. He was there watching as God created the first man. He was witness to God taking a rib from the man's side and making Eve. He hated God, and he hates us. That is who our enemy is. It is none other than that old serpent, Satan. He uses people to hurt other people.

When we operate from a place of woundedness, our thoughts are skewed, our motives are misplaced, and we can be overcome by the toxicity of bitterness.

Sarcasm springs from the heart of an individual with a wounded spirit. If you have a tendency toward sarcasm or criticism, you are operating from a place of woundedness. Left unchecked, it will fester and corrupt your entire heart, mind, soul, strength, and will. God specifically tells us what to do with such actions: put them away! He tells us that these things have no place in the life of a Christian (Ephesians 4:31; Colossians 3:8; 1 Peter 2:1). So what are we to do? Give our hurt to God, and allow Him to heal us. My healing took many years of me continually giving my pain and hurt to Him, over and over again.

It is possible to remember the event (no matter how painful) without the pain attached. This one took me a while. I had difficulty separating the offense from the offender. I viewed them as being one and the same.

One day, I went to my "fallen log altar" in the woods behind our house. I had been having a difficult time with the thoughts in my head. I was wanting to get revenge, wanting to hurt those who were hurting me, and I knew that those thoughts did not belong in the mind of a Christian. I sought God day and night about my attitude. As I knelt at that old log, God taught me a valuable lesson using a mud puddle and an earthworm. It had rained earlier in the morning, and the forest floor was soaking wet. There was a mud puddle, just on the other side of the log from where I was kneeling. I took no notice of it at first, for the heaviness in my heart drove me into prayer. Right in the midst of my tears and pain, God spoke. I heard Him say, "Look, look, look."

I opened my eyes, and my attention was drawn to that mud puddle. I thought it strange that God would want me to look at a puddle of muddy water, but the lesson was about to begin. I noticed something moving nearby the puddle and recognized a common earthworm crawling on the surface of the ground. It was making its way toward the mud puddle. I heard God say, "Watch, watch, watch." I watched as that earthworm crawled into the puddle and disappeared. I could not see the earthworm, but I could see the water rippling a bit as it made its way through. I was captured by the moment and continued to stare at the puddle, not certain of the outcome. Then I saw the earthworm emerge from the puddle. I had expected it to have mud all over its body. After all, it had just crawled through the mud puddle. That earthworm was clean. God spoke to me and said, "Just as I have brought this earthworm through a muddy environment clean, so I will bring you through the toxic place that you are in, and I will keep you clean by my Word that lives in you."

I cannot tell you that my thoughts were immediately clean and wholesome, but I can tell you that I have never forgotten that lesson there in the woods. None of us can live a supernatural life through natural endeavor. It takes the Holy Spirit in us to live a holy, God-honoring life.

Even when your perpetrator dies, that does not mean you are automatically free from the pain they caused you. This was true in my case. For years, long before her passing, I had dreams of my offender going over a cliff in a car and crashing on the jagged rocks far below. The vehicle she was riding in burst into flames upon impact, and I stood at the top of the cliff, rejoicing that the person who had been the source of so much pain could never hurt me again! These dreams troubled me, and I talked to my pastor about my concern. I told him that, sometimes, I enjoyed the dream so much that I felt like I was not even saved. I would have the dream and then repent for hours, asking God to forgive me and renew my mind. I felt like my mind was dirty. I prayed that those dreams would just go away.

When I learned that she had actually passed away, just a few years ago, I thought those dreams would stop. They didn't. They became nightmares or what I refer to as night terrors! They were always the same. They would start out with me living in the past, under her roof, and she would be chasing me all through the house with a knife! I would be screaming and running for my life! Just as she reached me, I would awaken! I experienced these nightmares for weeks after her death. I was so sleep-deprived I could barely function! I dreaded nighttime and could not sleep during the day. My body was a wreck, my nerves were shot, and my mental state of mind was not in a good place. I cried out to God and asked Him what on earth this was about.

After much prayer and fasting, God revealed that I had a trust issue that needed to be dealt with. I didn't trust God completely, even though I told Him I did. The problem I had was I told God I trusted Him, and then I would add a *but* to the sentence. That word *but* negates everything that was said before it. *But* and *trust* do not belong in the same sentence. Either I trust God with it all or I don't trust Him at all. I was crushed to think that God would see that in me. After all, He has brought me through, and the place He has brought me to, and there was still a problem with me choosing to fully and unreservedly trust Him. Trust means that I let go of the control, I no longer get to decide how or when; I simply let go and trust. I repented, pouring my heart out to God, and asked Him to forgive me, cleanse me, wash me, renew my mind, and grow me in the area of trust. Then I chose to trust Him. No more struggle, no more debate, simply trust. I leaped off the ledge of my own making, into the arms of my heavenly Father, completely trusting Him to catch me, and He did. Oh, He did!

In His embrace, I asked God to cleanse every painful memory, washing it clean with the water of the Word (Ephesians 5:26). I asked Him to help me forgive what I could not forget. I wanted to be done with this, once and for all! No more would the enemy toy with my mind, no longer would he torment me, or taunt me with accusations. My victim mentality had to go in the name of Jesus! The years of pain melted away into a peace that is beyond words.

God did it! He washed away, eliminated, erased every trace of pain associated with every memory of my past. The nightmares immediately ceased! For the first time since 1974, I was free! I was healed. I was whole. At last, I am ready to move to my next assignment! I walk in wholeness, no longer broken.

And the thing is, it is not about me at all. It is all about God. He is moving me into a new era and area of ministry. It will look different, sound different, and be different than anything I have done before. He is calling me to a ministry of deliverance and restoration, and I might even get to sing once in a while. I love how God works! He is so amazing. Even as I write, I feel the presence of God in these words. Glory to God!

God doesn't always block hardship from our pathway. He allows trouble and pain because He knows what it will take for us to look to Him, to seek

Him with all our heart, mind, soul, and strength! When we turn our eyes upon Jesus and look fully into His wonderful face, then He will use our pain to fulfill His purpose. But we must relinquish that pain to Him. No pain is ever wasted when we fully give it to God and allow Him to bring healing through the process.

When we hold on to hurt, we hinder our growth in God. He says He is our burden bearer, and He tells us to cast our burdens on Him. I prayed for years for God to take the heavy weight of wounded-ness I was carrying around, but nothing happened. The problem was, I had to let go and lay my hurt at His feet. He was not going to take something away from me that I was carrying around like a mountain on my back. It wore me right out, but I stubbornly held on to it and wore it like a medal of honor around my neck. It was never mine to carry, and it crushed me. Only God has the strength to carry our hurts, but He won't just take them, we have to give them to Him, lay them willingly in His lap, surrender them to Him, and trust Him with the outcome.

What hinders us from laying our burdens at His feet? Pride. Pride says we're our own provider, and we know better than God does how to handle life's messes. God is our Creator. He knows our frame. He is intimately acquainted with our grief. He wants to heal us, but we hold on to it as though, somehow, we can muddle through unscathed. The truth is, when we decide to be our own provider, we become a hindrance to our own healing. We stand in the way of God's provision—His grace and mercy. He is a perfect gentleman and will not take what we are not willing to release to Him. Cast your cares on Him, for He cares for you (1 Peter 5:7). He is our Waymaker, miracle worker, promise keeper, light in the darkness, and we can trust Him. He is our only hope. He is our very present help in trouble. He is more than enough!

I lived as a peacekeeper, not a peacemaker. There is a huge difference. I was not creating an atmosphere of peace. I was attempting to keep the peace at any cost. My own survival depended on keeping the peace. No matter that I was wounded, I needed to control the atmosphere to avoid conflict because conflict caused me more hurt and pain. Peace was my safe place, so I tiptoed around issues. I made a habit of telling myself that everything was all right when dysfunction reigned supreme. I went against what I knew in my heart and tried to convince my brain that all was well in paradise. And that stinking thinking got me into a lot of turmoil and pain.

Every one of us has been hurt. God tells us that offenses will come. As we traverse the path of life, we bounce into people who are operating from a spirit of woundedness. They lash out and hurt others wherever they go because of what is governing their heart and mind. Being a Christian does not exempt us from operating in a spirit of woundedness. Offenses happen, and when they do, we must be ready to deal with them, recognize them for what they are (an attack of the enemy), give them immediately to God, and not allow the offense to get a toehold in our soul. The enemy gains entrance through hurts, and once he slips through, he wreaks havoc in our minds. He is very well aware of our weak spots, and he will hone in on them. He does not strike us at our strongest place. He goes for the vulnerable areas and strikes over and over.

"Any overemphasis of any one particular spiritual truth becomes spiritual error" (Kathryn Kuhlman). When one truth is overloaded, it becomes a control issue and ushers in a Jezebel spirit. If you do not have spirit and truth operating together, you have nothing! Spirit without truth—you blow up; truth without Spirit—you dry up; put the two of them together as Jesus says to do, and you will grow up. Many are deceived and do not even know it.

Every one of us has a calling in our life. God planned it that way. He has a purpose for everything that He does. As you walk out your calling, you might find people disappearing from your inner circle. These people might be close friends who have been with you for most of your journey. But now God is calling you to a higher calling, a deeper walk, and a more powerful anointing. You will go places that they cannot follow because your calling is not their calling. Your time of preparation will look different than mine.

Do not compare your gifts, calling, and talents with anybody else's. God has placed inside of you exactly what He desired. He takes joy over who you are. Live in an attitude of gratitude for who you are and for God who lives inside you.

I have learned that no time spent with God is ever wasted! I cannot emphasize this enough! Jesus said, "Draw nigh to God, and He will draw nigh to you" (James 4:8). Linger in His presence, sit at His feet, become a student of the Word, for it is healing to your body (Proverbs 4:20–22). Fall in love with Jesus all over again.

Set your priorities in order. Prioritize your schedule. It is so easy, in fact, it is the plan of the enemy for us to become so busy with legitimate things that we crowd out the most important one. God must be first on the list. If you are investing more time, energy, and thought in anything or anyone else, then He is taking a back seat. His heart's desire is to see all His children walking in total victory, healed, delivered, whole, and to be equipped to do His bidding. There is a world full of hurting and lost souls who need what you have to give them. And I don't mean that you must be a preacher, pastor, teacher, or leader, but you will preach; we all preach. Everyone who has trusted Jesus Christ as Savior and made Him Lord of their life has a message to tell to the world. God is serious about this. He needs us to step up. He is calling each of us to seek Him first, to make Him our top priority. He is calling us to catch His vision and to see the lost through His eyes. He needs warriors who are all in. You will preach, and, sometimes, you will even use words.

Stay hungry for God! Stay thirsty for His presence! Embrace a lifestyle of worship, for it must be more than an event; it must become a lifestyle!

Your mission will look different than mine, for I can only fill my own shoes, and you are called to only walk in yours. God has a plan to use each of us in His own unique way, and when we commit to Him, He will bring us to the next assignment.

We are responsible to steward the gifts, calling, and talents He has given us.

Walk in humility before your God. I have no merit outside of Jesus Christ. I am humbled that God would devote so much energy in translating me into a vessel fit to carry the anointing. He could've looked at me fifty years ago and chosen to leave me in the mess that I created as a result of poor choices. But without harshness or condemnation, He lovingly guarded my life and gently led me to a dark place where He could get my undivided attention. Then, and only then, my training could begin.

Moses spent eighty years in God's school of training before He was ready to lead the nation of Israel out of Egypt. Joseph was in training from age seventeen to thirty before God placed him in a position of authority and responsibility. I have been in God's training camp for nearly fifty years, and now I see some glimpses of light shining through. Little shimmers have shone through as people have come forward to deliver messages from God for me. I will soon be emerging from the darkroom, fully developed, ready to shine in the Light!

Nobody is so broken that God cannot mend them.

If your rambunctious three-year-old were playing in the front yard and, suddenly, made a mad dash toward a very busy highway, would you not do everything within your power to stop that little one before they got hit by a vehicle? Of course, you would. You would run to their rescue out of love and concern but also out of discipline that would show them the danger of that decision. God is that way with us when we stubbornly choose to do our own thing. He sees what lies ahead of us in the path we have chosen, and He sometimes disciplines us harshly, not to hurt us, but to save us from ourselves and our own destruction.

If you are like me, you might not understand why your parents acted the way they did. Let me point out that there are no perfect parents, and often they raise us amid their own unresolved trauma. They might not understand us because they do not have the capacity to do so. You might feel that they have been emotionally unavailable to you, but that is because their parents were emotionally unavailable for them. And remember that our parents raised us through their own struggles, worries, pain, and fears.

When truth hits you square in the face, you become accountable to God for how you handle that truth. If you reject it, you will suffer the consequences of that error, and it could be harsh and hard to bear. If you accept it, embrace it, and allow it to change you into a more Christlike individual, then you have what I call a win-win situation. God wins, you win, and the world around you wins. To the degree that you are walking (or not) in all the fullness of the Holy Spirit, you are robbing your family, friends, coworkers, and everybody else of God's best for them. For it is only when we walk in all of His fullness that we can be the blessing to the world that God intends us to be. Anything less is just that, and who wants to be a less than?

You will know that you are ready to emerge from the darkroom of development when you no longer feel the need to promote yourself. If you are ready to come bursting out of that place with the single objective to bring absolute glory to God, and not to yourself, then you are probably developed to the point where God can now entrust you with your next assignment. Joseph was in prison with the king's baker and cupbearer. As you will recall, each of them had a dream of which Joseph was able to give an accurate interpretation. When those men were taken from the prison, Joseph called out to them and told them to remember him to the king when they stand before him. But they did not remind the king about Joseph, and he lingered there for years. Why? Because Joseph was still trying to control the outcome, still attempting to be his own provider, his own protector, his own power. So God had to allow him to stay in the dark for a few more years until he had gotten over himself and that self-promoting idea.

I often think about why I had to be in the darkroom for so long, and I am convinced that the reason was due to my stubborn mindset and way of thinking and that I did not realize the error of my ways. God knew what He had placed inside of me and the anointing that He placed on me, and He also knew that I was not in a place of spiritual maturity where I could carry it well. He knew that I would mess up, so He gently plucked me up and carried me to the darkroom, under His careful watch, nurturing and encouraging me to grow in Him. Wow! I am so grateful for every lesson, every correction, every moment of chastising, for in those moments, God showed His greatest measure of love and patience toward me.

Perhaps you have questions about how I managed to hold on for so long when things and situations went from bad to worse! I assure you I am not special. God inside of me is special. When He adds His SUPER to our natural, we become unstoppable in our faith! It was nothing short of determination on my part. I placed my faith in God's sovereign goodness. It was a choice. Faith is like a muscle; the more we exercise it, the more it increases in size and strength. When all I had was stripped away, and I stood in absolute humility before God, He did not condemn. He never gave up on me. I've often pondered why He didn't kick me to the curb and move on to someone who was not as broken. I believe it's because He is true to Himself. The Bible says God knew us before we were formed in our mother's womb. He knew me, He chose the gifts He would place inside me. He chose my hair color, the tone of my skin, gave me my voice, chose how tall I would be, gave me the desire to seek Him at a tender age, and He knew He could trust me with the call He placed on my life.

It would take me a while to get there, but He is not in a hurry, so He patiently waited for me to grow up and develop. I believe God doesn't give up on us because of the investment He deposits into each of us, even before we are born. He watches over His word to perform it (Jeremiah 1:12). There will always be difficult things that we face in every season, and God desires to use every single one of them to develop our character.

Never loathe the darkroom, for it is a very necessary place for development and advancement in the kingdom of God. Lean into the experience, trust God completely amid the dark, seek Him with all of your heart, and allow His Holy Spirit to complete the work that He started in you. Stand firmly on the promise that God gave you to be ALL you need and more! He is more than enough! So stand on the promise and continue through the process so you can be given your next promotion!

About the Author

MARILYN AND HER HUSBAND, DAVID, WILL CEL-
EBRATE twenty-one years of marriage this year.
Together, they have three children, five grandchil-
dren, and two great-grandchildren.

Marilyn is widely known for her singing voice
and has recorded several CDs, one of which con-
tains all original songs that she has written. But if
you ask her, she would tell you that she is a speaker
who sings; not a singer who speaks.

Her passion is teaching, speaking, and encouraging others on the journey of life. Her deepest desire is
for this book to bring God the greatest glory possible.

If you would like to have Marilyn as a speaker at
your church or event, please contact her at 8 Queen
Avenue, Shamokin Dam, Pennsylvania, 17876,
(570) 743-0402.